The Guru'Guay Guide to Uruguay

Beaches, Ranches & Wine Country

Karen A Higgs

2018

GURU'GUAY

D1722327

Guru'Guay Productions
Montevideo, Uruguay

Cover illustrations: Matias Bervejillo

FEEL THE LOVE

**The Guru'Guay website and guides
are an independent initiative**

Thanks for buying this book and sharing the love

Got a question? Write to info@guruguay.com

www.guruguay.com

To Sally Higgs, who has enjoyed beaches in the Caribbean, Goa, Thailand and on the River Plate

I started Guru'Guay because travellers complained it was virtually impossible to find a good guidebook on Uruguay. I later discovered why. The guidebooks published by the big companies were written by people who flew in for a few weeks and then left.

I'm British but I've been living in Latin America for more than half my life and moved to Uruguay in 2000. I'm also a professional musician, so I have close ties to music and culture here. In 2016 I wrote *The Guru'Guay Guide to Montevideo,* the first indepth English-language guidebook to the capital, based on my experience of **fifteen years living right here** in the capital.

But I knew that **most travellers who come to Uruguay want to spend some time at the beach, sample the great wine and maybe experience gaucho country**, besides checking out the unique culture and architecture of Montevideo.

Like so many of my fellow city-dwellers in Montevideo, I was really unfamiliar with the interior—the Uruguayan countryside. A musician colleague was hired to play in a folclore band and started gigging at country festivals attended by literally thousands every single weekend. Despite being born-and-bred in Uruguay, he had had absolutely no idea that this vibrant music scene outside of Montevideo even existed. And I'll confess, I was a beer woman before I started writing for Guru'Guay in 2014.

So I had to explore the interior and spend time talking to wine lovers and exploring different wineries. And my campaign began to track down great hotels and restaurants that open all year round at the beach (most beach hotels close down off season).

The Guru'Guay Guides are not endless dry lists of things to do and places to stay (as one Amazon reviewer perceptively noted). **They have passion and soul**.

The guide that you have in your hands is **the result of over a year of research**.

As a traveller, you have limited time. So **the Guru selects only the very best or the most curious** places to check out—so you can have **the most unforgettable holiday ever** and the planning is **stress-free**.

— *Karen A Higgs, aka The Guru*

Table of Contents

Read this first

Before you dive in, take a minute to read my criteria for what's in and what's not in this guidebook.

Which beaches are in this guide?

I've chosen a very varied range of beaches including **hippie-chic beaches in Rocha** closest to Brazil, glitzy **well-established beaches in Maldonado** and **nostalgia-inducing beaches closer to Montevideo**. Though not primarily beach destinations, the capital Montevideo and UNESCO heritage site Colonia del Sacramento are included in the chapters devoted to beaches (though truth be told they do have lovely beaches).

How did Guru'Guay select the ranches?

On the advice of several experts on rural tourism born-and-bred in the Uruguay interior themselves, I travelled the country and selected **seven estancias. They go from an extremely rustic ranch** owned by a gaucho couple who make ends meet by taking in visitors (they love to show you how they live) **to the grand estancia** of an Austrian-Uruguayan family with a lovely pool and capybaras in the garden **to a million-star vegetarian inn specialising in exciting horse rides**, set in an alternative life-style community in the stunning hills of Rocha. You can choose the one, or two or three that best suit your dream holiday. Every single owner told me that guests arrive and don't leave the estancia their entire stay so I have just included one or two sight-seeing recommendations on the way to or from each.

And the vineyards?

This book does not include every Uruguayan vineyard, nor every wine region. In consultation with experts, I visited **ten wineries in Uruguay's three most prominent wine-producing regions**. There are two small rule-breaking vineyards on the coast, perfect to pair with a beach holiday. Four vineyards clustered together in Carmelo, a rural town in western Uruguay, making it simple for you to organise your own three-night wine immersion programme (so to speak). The four vineyards just minutes outside Montevideo are all radically different—from Uruguay's most popular fine wine producer with vineyards in Uruguay and France to a family concern that offers yoga under the full moon followed by wine-tasting. **For the dedicated wine traveller** there are **two lists of the best Uruguayan wines** compiled by local connoisseurs to use to put together your own itinerary.

Guru'Guay only includes businesses open all year round

At the beach, **Uruguay has a very short high season** from Christmas to February. And what is almost unbelievable is that **many restaurants and hotels open for a mere handful of months**. How do they do it? I hate to admit it but the reality is, by radically overcharging their customers during peak season (see *Beaches, When to visit*). Guru'Guay is part of a movement to make Uruguay's tourism market better value for visitors and better for the country and its job market as a whole. We want travellers to have a wonderful holiday here all year round and we want you to have a choice of great hotels and places to eat at appropriate prices whenever you come. That's why in this book **we only include businesses that stay open all year round**.

Guru'Guay only recommends businesses striving for great service

Guru'Guay only includes establishments that provide **consistently excellent service whether they are high or low end**. The hotels included here were chosen because they have excellent online reviews from actual guests and then we went and checked them out for ourselves. **If we include a place where the offering is inconsistent but there was something else we love** about it, **we'll warn you**. The restaurants we selected after extensive research including consultations with chefs and local gastronomy experts. To be honest there was one point when I got desperate trying to find **great restaurants staying open all year round at the beach**. Then I got really lucky. I was introduced to people in the slow food movement. Chefs and establishments that prioritise the freshest, seasonal ingredients and who are reclaiming native fruit and fish. Places like Macachín, a tiny little 18-seater bistro in an urban backstreet fifteen minutes from Punta del Este run by an ex-motorbike mechanic whom chefs are saying is the most exciting thing to hit Uruguay culinarily in years. I am really excited to give these intrepid souls the visibility they deserve.

We're going native where terminology is concerned

I'll be using **terminology as used in Uruguay so that you'll be easily understood** when you are here. We'll refer to seasons as they are lived here so summer is December to February (see *Practical Tips, When to visit).* However as the vast majority of Guru'Guay readers are from the USA, temperatures are in Fahrenheit. We'll refer to the location of places as Uruguayans do. Ocean beaches are technically north of the capital but Uruguayans always refer to beaches being in the east—signposts on the highway will point you 'Al Este' (To the East). And we'll refer to 'rutas' rather than highways, kilometres rather than miles (I'll use miles in descriptions but locations will be indicated by their kilometre marker, so that you can follow road signs).

Grab yourself some free Uruguayan tourist maps

Excellent free paper maps are provided at all departmental tourist information centres in Uruguay and I recommend you get your hands on those when you get to a new department (as the provinces are called here). They are much better than anything we can include here. If you bring your phone or tablet, downloading a map (like GoogleMaps) is also handy. Gas stations stock maps. There is **free wifi all over Uruguay**[1] so you can keep roaming charges low.

A paper guidebook with online updates

Because we're based in Uruguay we can keep you up to date with any updates to this book's content post-publishing. Visit the Guru'Guay website[2] before you travel.

You can support Guru'Guay

We are an independent initiative promoting Uruguay to intrepid travellers who prioritise off-the-radar destinations. **Please support us by mentioning you came via Guru'Guay** when you contact any of the carefully-selected providers in this book.

---

1   Even the buses have free wifi in Uruguay www.guruguay.com/free-wifi-in-uruguay
2   www.guruguay.com/uruguay-guide-updates

Beaches

Uruguay has a population of just three million. During the summer the number doubles. The vast majority of visitors are from Argentina—many of whom have holiday homes here—followed by Brazilians who love the safety a holiday in Uruguay offers. This not a recent phenomenon. **Uruguayan beaches have been hugely popular tourist destinations for over a century** especially with Argentinians. The Hotel Argentino, an art-Deco gem which still dominates the Piriapolis promenade, was the largest and most glamorous resort in the whole of South America when it was built in the 1920s. **North Americans and Europeans make up just one in ten visitors** so you're in the vanguard.

The different beach areas in Uruguay

The wildest beaches are in the department of Rocha on the Atlantic coast closest to Brazil. These beaches were isolated and frequented solely by locals until a trickle of intrepid Argentinian backpackers started arriving in the 1990s. In the last few years Punta del Diablo and La Pedrera have become party towns for younger Argentinians and Brazilians around New Year but there's always ample space on the beach if you just walk fifteen minutes from the town centre. The vibe at most *Rochense* beaches is kind of hippie.

The most well-established beaches with the best infrastructure are in the department of Maldonado. Punta del Este is probably the most famous beach resort in South America after Rio de Janeiro, full of highrises and a frenetic summer scene. La Barra is hipper with surfing competitions and art galleries. Jose Ignacio, a tiny semi-rural peninsula with 28 permenant residents, has become the vacation choice of an international jet-set—think Mark Zuckerberg. If Punta is glitzy and La Barra hippie-chic, Jose Ignacio inclines to the haute-hippie.

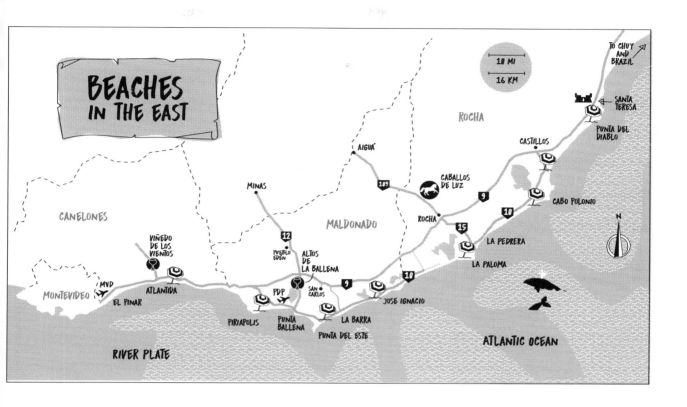

Beaches in the department of Canelones have a kind of nostalgic fifties summer air to them. Sleepy towns and simple pleasures. Middle-class Uruguayan families own holiday homes here passed from generation to generation. A vacation in these towns feel like you have been transported back to the kind of holidays you might have had when you were a kid.

I've included **Montevideo**, **Colonia** and **Carmelo**, not because I am suggesting you visit them specifically for a beach holiday. In fact Uruguayans opening this book will be surprised to see them included in the beach index. But while you are taking in the culture and architecture of Montevideo or swigging wine in Carmelo, why not take advantage of the beaches, right?

The ocean, the 'sea' and the River Plate

Let's talk briefly about the type of water you'll encounter at the different beaches. The beaches in Rocha and a large proportion of Maldonado are on the ocean (you will see highways signs to the 'Costa Oceánica'). The Atlantic Ocean officially starts at Punta del Este though east of Piriapolis all the beaches feel absolutely oceanic. Beaches between Montevideo and Piriapolis are technically on the estuary of the River Plate. But everyone—absolutely *everyone*—calls the water "el mar", the sea. It's understandable. There are waves and the river stretches as far as the eye can see. Indeed it takes over two hours by high speed hydrofoil to get to the other side. The water changes all the time from hour to hour. Sometimes it is green and salty like the sea, sometimes it's brown[3] like the river. Other times you literally see green and brown stripes intermingling. Pretty cool. In Colonia, the river has narrowed considerably— Buenos Aires can be seen on the horizon on a clear day—and the water is undoubtedly the river.

How long to stay

During the summertime if you have two weeks for a beach holiday my recommendation would be to pick two departments and stay a week at one beach and a week at the other. The distances in Uruguay are relatively short, so you can explore surrounding beaches quickly and easily.

You know how people say that by the time they have gotten into holiday mode, it's time to go home? For some reason, Uruguay's laid-back rhythm seems to sink in almost straight away. Maybe it's the lack of street lighting in many beach towns... but you'll find you'll sleep late, go to the beach, get some lunch, have a siesta, go back to the beach late afternoon, hang out, shower, dine and so it goes. If you're usually the antsy type, prepare yourself. You may find yourself unable to move from your sun lounger. And then it will be time for a sundowner.

---

3   The river is brown because it is very mature and carrying silt in suspension.

When to visit

Warmest weather Beaches are good for swimming and sunbathing from November till April and even occasional days the rest of the year. I took my uncle to La Paloma in May and we went swimming every day in glorious sunshine.

Avoid high season and peak season See *Practical Tips, When to visit, High season*

What you need to know

Accommodation prices skyrocket during high season In the most popular small resorts (Jose Ignacio, Punta del Diablo, La Barra and La Pedrera) accommodation rates can triple and even quadruple. Get the best rates by going to the beach before mid December or from March onwards (excluding Easter). Check out these actual rates in dollars (their spelling not ours) on a Jose Ignacio hotel website.

2016/2017	High Season December 15 trough December 25	New Year from December 26 to January 5	High season from January 6 to February 28	Out of Season From September 30 to March 31
Special Ocean View	Us$ 600	Us$ 1200	Us$ 600	Us$ 300
Superior Ocean View	Us$ 500	Us$ 1000	Us$ 500	Us$250
Junior Suite	Us$ 400	Us$ 825	Us$ 400	Us$ 200

Many hotels close down between May and September As demand outstrips supply, hotels can make a killing in high season. And then close down. The example above opens for just half the year. This is bad for travellers. And it's bad for the job security of the locals. The wonderful places we have found offer outstanding service—in no small measure as a result of their commitment to employing the same staff year in year out, all year round. In beach towns where we were not able to find a hotel that fulfilled our criteria (see *Read this first*), we recommend renting.

Off season beach restaurants may open on weekends only Most restaurants at the beach open from October to April. Those that stay open between May and September may operate on a reduced schedule from Friday dinner to Sunday lunch and public holidays. Public holidays will usually include Argentine, and occasionally Brazilian public holidays, besides Uruguayan.

Contacting restaurants via Facebook We have included opening times but they can change. Many Uruguayan businesses prefer a Facebook page which they'll keep well-updated to a website. A Facebook message is usually a very quick way to find out if your favourite resto is open.

How do you say beach in Spanish? The word for beach in Spanish is *playa*—pronounced ply-zhah by Uruguayans.

Renting a beach house

Most Uruguayans rent houses when they go to the coast rather than stay at hotels. There's accommodation for all styles, from luxury condos to rustic cabins. You can get great deals off season.

Minimum stay during peak season Before Airbnb came along house owners dictated rental conditions, such as imposing a minimum two-week stay in January and February. The internet and the consequent internationalisation of the Uruguayan rental market means things are changing. It still may not be possible to rent a large house for less than a week in January however a quick look online shows numerous beach rentals available for a single night. Sought-after locations like Cabo Polonio appear to have three-night minimums.

Ranchos At the beach a typical beachhouse is known as a *rancho*. It is NOT a ranch but something more akin to a rustic cabin. Especially in Rocha many *ranchos* are constructed from little more than wood and corrugated iron which will shelter you from the elements but that's about it. Some *ranchos* have electricity or running water, others do not. Some *ranchos* have a fridge running from a gas bottle. More basic places may just have a beer cooler and your butter will be floating around in the melting ice.

Going off the grid is a rare luxury these days and it is a joy to wake and sleep according to the rising and setting of the sun. This can be incredibly rewarding— as long as it's what you're expecting.

Cleanliness in a holiday rental or a rancho is not a given. I adore staying in a rancho but cannot count the number of times that the first thing I had to do when I arrived was to clean the place. Dirty windows, dirty fridge, dust everywhere. It adds insult to injury when you are paying WAY too much for a place this rustic just because of its privileged spot during peak season. If this is something that will really bother you, read reviews very carefully or choose off season.

Communicating with owners Your host will invariably be super friendly and communicative, but she may communicate in Spanish. She will expect you to write back in English. Make technology and Google Translate work and sort out your needs over email BEFORE you arrive.

Bedding and towels Typically beach rentals expect the client to bring their own bedlinen and towels. Check if linen is included. If it is not, contact your host to see if they will provide (or in the worse case "rent") the items.

Supplies You'll be expected to provide your own supplies—toiletries, toilet paper, insect repellent etc.—especially if you stay more than a few days.

OK, enough of the preparation. Let's get to the beaches.

Punta del Diablo, Rocha

Punta del Diablo is a fishing town with dirt roads, brightly-painted cabins and sweeping unspoiled beaches a few miles from the Brazilian border. It was founded by the Rocha family who came to the area in 1935 in search of good sea air for one of their children who suffered asthma. Around 1942, fishermen from nearby Valizas came to fish *tiburón* (shark). Shark's liver oil was a lucrative export. The only way to reach inland was by horse and cart which was pretty arduous as any tracks made in the dunes were quickly removed by the wind. The first road was built in 1968.

The Lonely Planet tapped Punta del Diablo as one of its Top ten Cities to visit in 2008 and the town has grown in size with a stable population of around a thousand though you can still cross the town in about an hour on foot. El Diablo—as townsfolk call it— previously attracted backpacker and hippie-types. Nowadays there's a wide range of accommodation from budget to luxury.

The beaches

The wonderful beaches stretching over six miles of coastline are utterly deserted most of the year. The Playa de los Pescadores (Fishermen's Beach) and Playa de Rivero are the closest to the centre of town. The Playa de la Viuda is named after the widow of an Argentine businessman who lived in the mansion at the far end of the beach which was built before the road into town existed. Many of the most ritzy condos overlook the Viuda. The Viuda and Rivero are frequented by surfers.

Things to do

Observing the fishermen on Playa de los Pescadores Fishermen's Beach is Punta del Diablo's iconic beach. Its calm waters are a favourite of families and it's where the artisanal fishing boats head off in the morning. The fishermen return just before sundown and heave the boats up onto the beach to offload and clean their catch. The fish is sold from the huts that line the main street.

Beach hike through Santa Teresa National Park A spectacular walk along some of the most beautiful beaches in Uruguay. Walk east along Playa Grande (an appropriately named very long beach), Playa del Barco and then Playa Achiras. Each beach is separated by rocky headlands though you can easily make your way along sandy stretches without footwear. To visit the fort you'll come to a small restaurant La Moza at the end of Playa Achiras. From there pick up the road that takes you the final twenty minutes inland to the fort. If you have the energy, nip over the headland to the next beach, Playa La Moza. Some say it's the one of the most beautiful in Rocha. The walk takes 2-2.5 hours one way. Take water, a snack, money (for lunch and entry to the fort), sunscreen and flip-flops or shoes to explore the park.

Whale-watching There is a wooden watching post at the end of Playa Grande. Some of the first whales of the 2015 season were spotted in Punta del Diablo in June—which was exceptionally early for the regular whale-watching season. Walking along Playa Grande we saw two whales just off the beach. We watched them for an hour before eventually moving on ourselves—leaving the whales behind.

A rainy-day trip to Brazil On a cloudy day, thousands of Uruguayans head to the Uruguay-Brazil border on a buying pilgrimage. On the Uruguayan side lies the town of Chuy (pronounced choo-wee), to the north of the main street the Brazilian town of Chui. Chuy is a typical border town—singularly unattractive with duty-free shops (you'll need your passport to be able to buy). What else is there to do in Chuy? Take a photo of yourself on main street with arms outstretched, one in Brazil and the other in Uruguay. Marvel at the eery accuracy with which your cellphone switches national providers every time you cross the main street.

What you should know

El Diablo Punta del Diablo too much of a mouthful? NEVER refer to Punta. Punta in Uruguay is always, but always Punta del Este. The in-crowd talk about going to El Diablo. If you're texting the acceptable local form is Pdd. Yup, just like that. Consider yourself in.

There is no static ATM The nearest are in Castillos and Chuy. So have back-up plans. During summer, mobile ATMs are brought in however they frequently run out of cash. Credit cards are accepted in most supermarkets and restaurants.

Building regulations prohibit highrises but unthinking developers have packed as many *cabañas* onto one plot as they can. The local government has not invested in infrastructure and when the town swells to over 30,000 in January the pressure on services is evident. As are the stiletto-wearing tourists from Brazil and Argentina picking their way through the pot-holed streets on their way to the glossy, neon bars, all of which will disappear come March.

When to visit

Avoid peak high season The crazy time of the year in Punta del Diablo is from Christmas Eve to January 10 when Brazilians and Argentinians come with family and friends to celebrate the holidays. In early January a deluge of twenty-something partiers hits the town with full force. February and the Easter week holiday see the return of Uruguayans so the vibe is more laid-back.

Off season between March and mid-December, Punta del Diablo goes back to being a sleepy seaside town with deserted streets and beaches.

Where to stay

Posada Lune de Miel

The sweetest red cabins picturesquely located around a small pool and bougainvillea and palm filled garden an eight minute walk from the beach. You're not too far from the town but far enough from the hubbub. Each cottage is cheerfully decorated, scrupulously clean with a basic but nicely designed kitchenette for preparing yourself coffee and simple meals. There's air conditioning and TV with cable. The owners, Uruguayan Natalia and her French husband Jean, both speak English and are the most friendly and helpful of hosts. They really go out of their way to make you feel at home and provide invaluable tips on short-cuts down to the most secluded beaches, the best places to eat and where to visit. There's no maid service and breakfast is optional, which helps keep prices excellent value especially off season. Bikes available for rent. Free transfer from the town centre. Write to Jean and Natalia at info@posadalunedemiel.com or visit www.posadalunedemiel.com $$

Pueblo Rivero

These stylish two-storey cottages perched on the hillside have panoramic ocean views from the living rooms and master bedrooms. Each cottage has its own outdoor grill with tables, benches and an all important hammock in which to swing and watch the ocean. Pueblo Rivero won a design award back in 2012. Interiors are clean and modern with an open fireplace. Mari the housekeeper keeps wood available and it's a delight to make a fire. An optional breakfast includes good strong coffee, freshly squeezed juice and warm pastries. The kitchen is slightly impractical in design. There's daily house-keeping. As the floors are polished cement, slippers recommended in the cooler months. Write to Pablo at info@pueblorivero.com www.pueblorivero.com $$$$

Where to eat

Il Tano Cucina

Run by Argentinian chef Luciano and his Montevidean partner Ximena, Il Tano is set in the pine forests about five blocks back from the ocean, in a gorgeous wooden house with a deck lit with candles in the evening. During the winter months, there's a roaring fire, the atmosphere is laid-back, many of the guests are clearly friends of the family and little ones fall asleep on the sofa in front of the fire. Specialities are home-made pastas and seafood. Luciano's kitchen garden provides most of the herbs and veggies and he forages for seaweed and mushrooms. Check out the *croquetas de sirí* and the fresh seaweed and ricotta raviolis in a cream and prawn sauce. They stock Uruguayan wines and craft beers. Open high season (Dec-Apr) daily noon-4pm 7pm-midnight; low season dinner daily 7-10pm Sat-Sun lunch.
Reserve with Ximena at info@iltanocucina.com

How to get to Punta del Diablo

Ruta 9 km 298. From La Paloma (1 h 30 m), Montevideo (4 h), Punta del Este (2 h 30 m)

Driving From Montevideo take the IB and R9 to km 298. R9 is a well maintained highway with abundant signage and almost deserted off season after the Punta del Este exit. Coming from La Pedrera, La Paloma or Cabo Polonio take R10 until you reach R9.

Bus 4.5 hours from Montevideo (COT, CYNSA and Rutas del Sol). You can also get there by bus from La Paloma, La Pedrera, Cabo Polonio and San Carlos (San Carlos is a connecting hub for beaches in Maldonado). A one-way ticket from Montevideo is about 600 pesos.

Santa Teresa National Park, Rocha

The Parque Nacional Santa Teresa is one of Uruguay's most beloved protected parks with over two thousand acres of forest and gardens, a well-restored colonial fort in verdant grounds and some of Uruguay's most spectacular and almost always deserted beaches. During the peak of high season the park is packed with campers. Come pre-peak and savour some of the best beaches in Uruguay all for yourself.

The fort and the park

The location of the Santa Teresa Fort was designated by the Portuguese in 1762 on the only rocky outcrop in an area dominated by dunes and wetlands, guarding a strategic route through the marshes to the sea. However it was the Spanish who finally built the fort which viewed from the air is an irregular pentagon. The thick yellow lichen-covered walls, four metres at the base tapering to two at the top, are visible from the highway and contrast dramatically with pristine green lawns. After falling into abandonment the fort was restored by the Uruguayan government in the 1920s and is one of the few surviving bastions of the colonial era on the continent. For a small entrance fee you can visit the armoury. Views from the parapet of the surrounding countryside and the ocean are stunning. Open Dec-March daily 10am-7pm, off season Wed-Sun 1-7pm.

Explore the park's forested areas, picnic, check out the beaches and birdwatch on the lakes. There's a rather over-run but very atmospheric tropical greenhouse and a *sombráculo* for subtropical plants both erected in 1939. The rose garden contains more than three hundred species. Children will love the hotchpotch collection of wild and domesticated animals but I confess I find it a little sad.

Where to stay

Santa Teresa is considered one of the best equipped camping areas in the country by local standards and at peak season receives … get ready… 12,000 campers. Camping is popular with young people. Sound equipment may get set up amongst the trees or loud music blasted at the beach. If you are a nature-loving camper definitely consider Santa Teresa—off season.

Where to eat

The park is run by the Uruguayan army and the soldiers live on site with their families. Many of the food areas are staffed by family members to supplement their income. At the petting zoo I had an amazing *torta frita* (typical street food). There are a few small supermarkets during high season serving the campers and restaurants, none of which stand out.

How to get to Santa Teresa

R9 km 306. Rocha (1 h 15 m), La Paloma (1 h 30 m), Punta del Diablo (15 m), Montevideo (4 h 15 m).

Driving From Montevideo take R9 to the km 306 marker.

Bus COT and CYNSA run from Montevideo, La Pedrera, La Paloma and Punta del Diablo.

Cabo Polonio, Rocha

Inhabited for thousand of years by indigenous tribes, legend has it that Cabo Polonio was named after one of the many ships that sunk off the rocky cape and her three treacherous islands in the 1700s. Attracted by the bounty to be had from ships bound for Spain laden with Latin American riches, the area became a hideout for pirates and smugglers. After the lighthouse was built in 1881 fishermen and seal trappers replaced the pirates. The fishermen remain though the trappers are no more after the government banned seal-hunting in 1992.

Photographer Stéphane San Quirce describes Polonio with enigmatic beauty as "a lost island between the Atlantic Ocean and a sea of sand dunes". It's not an island but it does feel like one, and it stands relatively unchanged since the days of pirates and smugglers. It's not what Cabo Polonio has—its huge deserted beaches, rocky islands heaving with baying seals, and tiny colourful shacks—but what it doesn't have that makes it unique. There's no electricity, no running water, no TV, no cars and no streets.

Polonio was designated a protected national park in 2009. You need to park your car at the visitors centre on the highway and ride an ancient safari-style double-decker truck through five miles of dunes. The ride is incredibly fun—thirty minutes bumping through dunes and then a glorious speed over Playa Sur with Cabo Polonio—with its tiny houses clinging to the cape and not a single tree to break the wind—growing ever closer. In summer you descend from the truck at a grass roundabout in the centre of the village into some kind of parallel hippie universe.

Narrow grassy paths fan out from the roundabout lined with wood-hewn shacks selling cold beer and fried seafood caught that morning run by stoic local women. Dread-locked travellers spread out their wares on colourful blankets, offering jewellery and crafts, tie-died beach wraps and to plait your hair for a few pesos. Someone's inevitably strumming a poorly-tuned guitar. And of course a legal joint is being passed around. Wend your way down to the water a minute away. The beaches are wild with pristine white sand. Even during high season there's always a piece of virgin sand to lie out on. Or head over to the iconic lighthouse to watch seals sparring feet away from where you are standing. You can cross the whole village in a matter of minutes and explore the whole place in a matter of hours.

What you should know

No electricity Since the area has become a national park no electricity is allowed, other than to power the lighthouse. Bring a head-light or torch. Trying to cook a meal by candle light or find your way home after a few beers is not easy.

No ATM Bring plenty of cash as most places do not accept credit cards or electronic payments. There is an ATM at the entrance of the national park but it is not always working.

Forget about your phone Nicer rentals have solar panels. Everywhere else is without electricity. A few businesses charge devices for a small cost however they may not always be open. Be prepared to essentially switch off.

Bring a few treats There is just one local shop which is surprisingly affordable and well-stocked considering everything has to be brought in over the dunes by truck. It has fresh fruit and vegetables and a good selection of booze. If you plan on cooking, familiarise yourself with opening hours and perhaps bring a few titbits with you. After all, you are on holiday.

If you can deal with the basic facilities and overlook the stress on those facilities during high season, what Polonio lacks it makes up for when the sun goes down. The scene is not about clubs and bars. It's about sitting around experiencing the joy of having less—a shared bottle of wine, a bonfire, new friends, your pigeon Spanish and the millions of stars overhead.

Things to do

Seal watching Uruguay has a seal population of a quarter of a million and most live on the three Torres Islands off Cabo. The majority are southern fur seals. One in ten are the much larger South American sea lions easily identifiable by their size and their huge manes—fishermen refer to them as "*pelucas*" (wigs). There's also the occasional Southern elephant seal—the males have huge proboscis resembling an elephant's trunk. Make your way over to the lighthouse. At the foot lies the seal colony which is lightly fenced off nowadays. The seals on Cabo Polonio itself are males which have been expelled from the islands by rivals. They are bidding their time to return which explains the persistent sparring. During breeding time in November and December so many thousands of males are expelled they spill over and occupy the entire tip of the peninsula. You'll be walking among them. They are big but they present no danger unless provoked. The rest of the year numbers vary but it's extremely rare not to see even a few seals.

Climb the lighthouse The coastline was so treacherous to shipping that the lighthouse was built in 1881. Its light is visible over twenty miles away. Counting the seconds between the flashes is a summer tradition. So much so that singer-songwriter Jorge Drexler (Uruguay's only ever Oscar winner) wrote a popular song called "Twelve seconds of darkness" (*Doce segundos de oscuridad*). Today the lighthouse is a national monument.

When to visit

Peak season From Christmas to mid-January thousands flock to Cabo Polonio. In the last few years the atmosphere of the centre of town has changed somewhat as older teens have moved in from other resorts en masse to sample Cabo's delights. Be aware that you are going to pay way over the odds in peak season for what that house is worth and ideally book well in advance. Read amenity details and reviewers comments carefully.

Low season Fall and spring are absolutely delightful. In the colder months Cabo Polonio takes on an almost Hebridean solitude. Perfect for a personal retreat if you revel in rusticity. Given that the weather can be unpredictable, don't book until you get to Uruguay. Check the weather forecast and plan your visit during one of those Indian summers that are so frequent (see *Practical Tips, When to visit*).

Where to stay

Cabo Polonio is tiny and the very limited hotel options (mainly hostels) do not meet the Guru'Guay criteria (see *Read this first*). I'd recommend renting a house like the locals do or visiting for the day. Rental options range from a few beautifully-decorated beach houses on the water to more numerous but basic *ranchos.*

Most *ranchos* in Cabo Polonio are constructed from little more than wood and corrugated iron. They will shelter you from the elements and get you back to basics. There is no electricity or running water. They will often be described as "rustic" and this will be no exaggeration. See *Beaches, Renting a beach house*

If you want to get well away from the city centre, consider a house off the peninsula. If you choose Playa Sur, when taking the truck in, ask the drivers to drop you off en route.

Where to eat

Spreading out from the central roundabout tiny shacks sell cold beer, seafood *empanadas* (pastry turnovers), delicious freshly-caught fish *milanesas* in a bread roll and the local speciality, *buñuelos de algas*. La Majuga and Lo de Dani are run by the wives of fishermen. There are a couple of more conventional-style restaurants right on the beach with lounge beds and hammocks. However they were closed for the winter when we went in late April meaning that they didn't make the cut for this book.

How to get to Cabo Polonio

R10 km 264.5 La Paloma (45 m), Punta del Diablo (50 m), Punta del Este (2 h), Montevideo (5 h)

Driving From Montevideo take R9 to Rocha, then Ruta 15 until km 5 and turn left onto R10. Drive to km 264.5. Park in the supervised carpark (apx. 200 pesos per day).

Bus CYNSA and Rutas del Sol run from Montevideo, San Carlos (connecting to Punta del Este) and other beaches in Rocha.

Buying truck tickets In summer trucks leave for Cabo every half hour or so between 7am-10pm and return between 8.30am-9pm. Off season there are just six inbound and outbound trips. Call as the timetable[4] may not be up to date. The last inbound truck of the evening waits for the last bus from Montevideo. The visitors centre is open 24 hours 365 days a year. Buy a ticket for the next truck and take a look around or grab something to drink from the small canteen. A two-way ticket costs a little over 200 pesos. Children under 5 travel free. Surf boards 100 pesos.

---

4   www.puertadelpolonio.com.uy/#horarios

La Paloma & La Pedrera, Rocha

There are several stories of how La Paloma which means 'the dove' got its name. One is that viewed from the top of the lighthouse the bay looks like a dove with its open wings. The more romantic story is that La Paloma, originally baptised Cape Santa Maria, was a point feared by sailors as the site of so many shipwrecks. Sailors would see the sea spray breaking over the rocks of the cape and flying in the air and visualise the white wings of a dove—and their potential demise, I suppose.

La Paloma is the biggest beach town in Rocha with almost four thousand people living there year round. It's the only beach in Rocha with any significant infrastructure—there a choice of hotels and restaurants, a small cinema, two casinos and a hospital. However this is not a smaller version of glamour puss Punta del Este. La Paloma is frequented by middle-class Uruguayans, many of whom have holiday homes, and the vibe is decidedly family-oriented.

The beaches

Each one of **La Paloma's beaches** has a different personality. Most of them are popular surfing spots. **Anaconda** is The surfer beach. It's miles long with different *bajadas* or paths down to the beach—Zanja Honda, Corumbá, Gavilán, Mar de la

Tranquilidad ("Mdt" pronounced emay-deh-teh by aficionados). **La Balconada** is La Paloma's 'chic' beach frequented by older teens though families are numerous too. There's a *parador* or beach-stand selling snacks and drinks, and music. **El Cabito** is a good whale-watching point with rock pools where locals collect seaweed for *buñuelos*. It's a good swimming spot. Beaches ideal for families with smaller children are Los Botes and Bahia Chica. **Los Botes** has a gentle slope down to the water, where the local fishermen pull up their boats and offload their catch early in the morning. **Bahia Chica** in a sheltered inlet facing Tuna island frequented by residents of the old part of town. **La Serena** is the most far-flung beach from the centre with lifeguard service heading towards the Laguna de Rocha. Like Anaconda it's wide with good waves for surfing, ideal for sports and long walks. The dunes that border the beaches are in reconstruction, so use the walkways provided.

From the port towards the east lie a string of wide beaches—**La Aguada**, **Costa Azul**, **Antoniópolis** (km 224.5) and **Arachania** (km 225.200). As settlements have expanded they have pretty much blended into each other. La Aguada and Costa Azul are separated visually by a high grassy dune—a great vantage point. Antoniópolis and Arachania are simpler neighbourhoods with ocean views. At the far end of the beach lies La Pedrera.

La Pedrera (km 228) is perhaps the greenest seaside town in Rocha perched on a rocky forested balcony overlooking two golden beaches. It used to be known as Punta Rubia, golden point. That's how sailors hailed its sands. Nowadays it's named after the six million year old baroque-style rock formations that divide Playa del Barco from Playa Desplayado. The younger set hang out at the Playa del Barco baptised after a shipwreck. The Desplayado is more family-friendly, less busy with calmer waters. With its *rambla* (promenade) and white-pillared promenade wall, La Pedrera feels more sophisticated than its homelier neighbour La Paloma. A number of its 200+ residents are émigré Argentine artists. Just outside of La Pedrera, a twenty-minute walk along the beach to the east lies the new **Punta Rubia** (km 230.3) which is greener and more isolated.

Things to do

Visit the La Paloma lighthouse The Cabo Santa Maria lighthouse built in 1874 is situated in the old part of La Paloma which you can appreciate from the top after climbing 150 steps. The lighthouse had a tragic beginning. The tower collapsed when it was near completion. Stories vary regarding the reason for the collapse. Perhaps it was because inexperienced builders used seawater to make the cement which cracked in a storm, killing seventeen of the mainly Italian workers. They were buried at the foot of the lighthouse and their graves can still be seen today. There's a small entrance fee. Children under 8 are not permitted. Open daily 10am-1pm and 3-6pm.

The classic Pedrera-Paloma beach walk takes you four miles (6 km) along the beach from one town to the other. If you are staying in La Paloma, La Pedrera is a great place to check out for restaurants. Those staying at La Pedrera could make the lighthouse their final destination.

La Pedrera high street La Pedrera has two landmarks—the rambla and a tall water tank (referred to as the *tanque de OSE* pronounced O-say, the name of the national water company). The high street runs from one to the other in a straight line. During the summer it's packed with restaurants, bars, bookshops, boutiques, clothing stores, marijuana-gear shops and a craft fair. Street artists abound. All this activity disappears off season. There's a colourful church, which has a bell rescued from a shipwreck inside.

Laguna de Rocha If there's one trip you must make while you are at the beach, make it this one. This huge lagoon stretches almost a far as the eye can see, and it's miraculously separated from the Atlantic Ocean by just a thin strip of sand. The lake is very shallow and host to a huge diversity of fauna including one of the world's largest flocks of black-necked swans, otters and capybaras. From February to May you can watch night-time shrimp fishing. The fishermen hold lamps close to the surface of the water and then scoop up the shrimp. It's a magical spectacle. During shrimp season the locals serve shrimp and beer from a brightly-painted hut. The rest of the year, you'll have to bring your own provisions. The lake is absolutely virgin with zero commercial development. Plan to spend at least half the day walking, swimming, bird-watching and experiencing the Uruguayan wetlands. Take plenty of sunscreen as there is very little shade. The walk takes about two hours from Los Botes along 3-4 miles of the best surfing beaches in Uruguay. By car the lake is about 15 km from La Paloma. Take R10 to the lake, the last 8 km are along dirt roads. Park at the shrimp ranch and then continue on foot. From Jose Ignacio, just keep going along R10 (about 40 km) till you reach Playa Del Caracol one kilometre from the lagoon and park.

Important note, you cannot cross the thin strip of land by car, even if the dunes have temporarily closed access of the lake to the ocean. The ecosystem is very delicate and proceeding by vehicle will land you with a hefty fine.

Day trip to Cabo Polonio See *Beaches, Cabo Polonio* In fact you can day trip to any beach in Rocha and beaches in Maldonado including Jose Ignacio (1.5 hours).

Horseriding in the hills of Rocha The Sierras of Rocha, one of the most picturesque hill ranges in Uruguay, is just an hour's drive from La Paloma. In the sierras lies a little gem of alternative tourism, where you can have a wonderful spicy meal with organic vegetables (time to detox from all that meat) and go for a spectacular horse-ride with the coolest English-speaking guides. Run by Lucie, the Caballos de Luz inn offers lunch and an adventurous afternoon ride. Lucie loves to cook Thai, Indian and Mexican cuisine. Tuck into a delicious three-course meal in the open air and have a swim in a crystalline river or a siesta in a hammock before you head off to the hills on horse-back. 65 USD. Contact Lucie at caballosdeluz@gmail.com. See *Estancias, Caballos de Luz*

When to visit

La Paloma and La Pedrera all year round Both resorts stay open for business all year round. La Pedrera Social Club holds free music and arts events off season.

Avoid peak high season in La Pedrera In the last few years La Pedrera has become very popular, attracting an influx of younger partiers. Lax enforcement of licensing laws has made the town centre very noisy, impossible for holiday makers who want to sleep at night. Unless you're planning to join the partiers, avoid renting within ten blocks of the centre of town from Christmas till January 10 and Carnival. For the rest of high season, La Pedrera goes back to being a very peaceful town.

Carnival in La Pedrera is the most popular carnival party on the Uruguayan coast. Nowadays this once neighbourhood parade has become a bit of a free-for-all. It's a massive party on the main street bringing together thousands of mostly young people, who dress up (very little effort goes into the costumes) and throw water all day, every day, especially on the Monday night of carnival. Bars play loud music all day and night. In 2015 20,000 people partied during carnival (twenty thousand, not a typo).

Winter solstice (*Fogatas de San Juan*) At the end of June, a new ritual has emerged in La Pedrera to commemorate the longest night of the year, promoted by locals fed up with the massification of Carnival. There's a bonfire and traditional Uruguayan *candombe* music and drumming in front of the Social Club.

What you should know

Fill up with gas in La Paloma. The ANCAP gas station on the corner of at Av. Del Puerto and Av. Solari is open 24 hours 7 days a week.

Getting cash (ATMs) There are three ATMs in La Paloma—one on the corner of Av. Solari and Titania streets, the other in Cambio Nelson, Av Solari and Av. Del Navio. There's also a a cash machine in the El Dorado supermarket but it does not always work. There is now an ATM in La Pedrera two and a half blocks from the R10 roundabout next to the INTI restaurant.

Where to stay

Both La Paloma and La Pedrera have a number of hotels ranging from luxury to budget. However none of them met the Guru'Guay criteria of consistently excellent online reviews (see *Read this first*).

Most Uruguayans rent houses and there are some lovely places to stay for all budgets. In La Paloma every neighbourhood is pretty different. Personally I prefer the pine-forested areas farther from the centre—Los Botes, Barrio Country and Anaconda. Surfers will find waves and cheapest accommodation in La Aguada or Costa Azul.

In La Pedrera pretty much anywhere is lovely to stay, especially off season, other than the centre during peak season.

Barrancas de Arachania, Arachania

Barrancas de Arachania is a small private neighbourhood of eight individually-designed vacation rentals—some of wood, others adobe, others more traditional—half way between La Paloma and La Pedrera in a secluded green glade a couple of blocks back from the beach. Thanks to clever design each house feels totally private and most have views of the ocean. We stayed at Ombu, a charming, well-equipped three bedroom house which has a comfortable living room with a fireplace and a dining room with sliding doors and an enormous indoor grill. Perfect for creating your own Uruguayan barbecue regardless of the weather. The caretaker Amanda is very helpful and a real character. She speaks very little English but makes herself understood. The owners are available on WhatsApp and email in English. There's a well-equipped supermarket five minutes walk away. One thing to be aware of is that the ocean is rough. There are lifeguards during high season but even experienced swimmers should take care when bathing. Overall this accommodation was much better than the average rental in this price bracket in Uruguay and there are great discounts for off season stays. Write to Martin and Jorge at info@pedrerapaloma.com.uy www.barrancasdearachania.com.uy $$-$$$$

Where to eat

La Pedrera has a reputation of having the best selection of high-end restaurants in Rocha but they only open in high season. Guru'Guay pays homage to those that stay open all year long. Choose the dishes we mention to ensure the best experience.

Don Rómulo, La Pedrera

Don Rómulo is a La Pedrera institution open daily. The Guru takes her hat off to chef Jorge and the team at Don Rómulo. Food can be variable but the home-made pasta is always excellent. Open daily noon-4pm, 8pm-midnight, weekends noon-midnight

Ay Candela, La Pedrera

A lovely Argentinian couple run this quaint little restaurant set back off the main street. The menu is limited with everyone loving the pizzas and the salads. If there are a lot of customers, the kitchen can be quite slow. Go prepared and not too hungry. Open daily in summer, off season from Friday dinner to Sunday lunch

La Pedrera Club Social y Deportivo, La Pedrera

The classic Pedrera social club cantina offers simple, home-made dishes—*milanesas*, pastas, fries. The speciality is *miniaturas* made from fish caught by Juan earlier in the day for just 150 pesos. It's one of the cheapest places on the coast. The club maintains an active social scene during the winter offering live music and cinema on weekends and really deserves support. Each year the concession is renewed. The husband-wife team in 2017 were Juan and Rosana. Open March-December Daily noon-8pm, later on Saturdays and Sundays as long as there are customers. The club becomes a discotheque during high season.

Las Rocas Restó, La Paloma

Las Rocas is on the main strip in La Paloma, a culinary oasis amidst the *chivito*-and-fries joints. It's a small restaurant that prioritises simple cuisine, fresh ingredients, generous portions, reasonable prices and the friendliest service. Run by owners Florencia and Martin since 2015, they've been steadily improving both the food and the locale but the good-natured service and the commitment to good cooking (their kitchen is on full view) have been there from the start. The menu prioritises local seafood in season—fresh fish, sirí crab and mussels. Try their *buñuelos de algas*—Martin forages the seaweed in the mornings before opening. The classic *milanesa de pescado* is big enough to share. There are delightful touches like a basket of throws for chilly evenings. Open daily in summer, off season from Friday dinner to Sunday lunch

How to get to La Paloma and La Pedrera

La Paloma **R15 km 0** Montevideo (3 h), Punta del Este (1 h 30 m), Punta del Diablo (1 h 30 m)
La Pedrera **R10 km 228** Same as above. Cabo Polonio (30 m)

Driving to La Paloma From Montevideo (240 km) along Ruta 9 to km 209, then Ruta 15 to km 0. From Punta de Este (120 km) take R10 until Jose Ignacio, take the Camino Ing. Sainz Martinez (picturesque paved road with lots of curves) until you reach R9. You can also take backroads from R10 to R9 which must be driven with caution. From Punta del Diablo (110 km) take the R9 highway and turn at km 209 to La Paloma. From Cabo Polonio (58 km) take R10—couldn't be easier!

Driving to La Pedrera La Pedrera is just 10 km east of La Paloma on R10. From Punta del Diablo (120 km) take R9 and turn at km 209 to La Paloma. From Cabo Polonio (48 km) take R10 west.

You can't drive along the coast from Jose Ignacio/Punta del Este Don't make the mistake we all do thinking that it's possible to drive along the R10 from Jose Ignacio to La Paloma. Though maps may show the road as unbroken, R10 disappears into sand and dunes and even open water depending on the time of year once you hit the Laguna de Rocha. There is a fine for attempting to cross in a vehicle.

Bus COT, CYNSA and Rutas del Sol run from Montevideo to La Paloma and La Pedrera daily (just over 3-4 hours depending on stops). Buses from other departments travel La Paloma. There are two local services—La Paloma-La Pedrera and the other La Paloma-Playa Serena.

Jose Ignacio, Maldonado

Though nowadays the likes of Elon Musk, Shakira and a Murdoch Jr have owned houses on this tiny peninsula just six blocks wide by six blocks long, like so many of the beach towns in Uruguay Jose Ignacio started out as a fishing village. Noone knows for sure who the original Jose Ignacio was, but as far back as 1763 there was an estancia by that name in the vicinity. Development came at snail's pace. In the 1970s electricity still hadn't reached the village and a square foot of land cost just one dollar. Today during high season a simple mid-century holiday home in this "haute-hippie hideaway" as one luxury travel writer called it can rent at 70,000 USD a week. Despite this, we're still in Uruguay. The streets are sandy and the service is slow and convivial. But there are chi-chi tea rooms, designer boutiques disguised as beach shacks, cube-like art galleries and a 'Valet Parking' sign at the beach.

Jose Ignacio has a permanent population of just three hundred—and just 28 on the peninsula—but on a peak season weekend eight thousand people can flood into town. Where do they all stay? With such demand on accommodation and street parking, development is creeping west. La Juanita is an adjacent forested *barrio* where some of the locals who can no longer afford the prices of Jose Ignacio are making their homes amongst the woodlands. Rentals—a mix of hippie-chic modernist chalets and colourful containers (houses made out of shipping containers are all the rage)—are more accessibly-priced and there are a number of good restaurants attended by their owners next door to locals' cottages surrounded by their barking dogs.

Strict regulations around building and commerce enforced by moneyed residents mean that Jose Ignacio is likely to extend its current status as the place to be for wealthy Europeans and North Americans into the future.

The beaches

The **Mansa** faces Punta del Este. The water is calm, the beach is fairly low-key and it's the place to watch the sun go down over the fishing boats pulled up onto the beach for the night. The **Brava** is to the east. In high season, its powerful waves and general cachet make it popular with surfers, supermodels and Argentine magnates. Just a mile along the generally deserted beach you reach Laguna Garzón.

Things to do

Jose Ignacio has everything on site that you need. Just add a good book. You may plan to do a whole bunch of things but are likely to end up just letting the days flow into one another.

Climb the Jose Ignacio lighthouse Watch out for treacherous gusts of wind. There's a rope to hang onto to help yourself up and down.

The Laguna Garzón Bridge The perfectly-circular Laguna Garzón Bridge was designed by Uruguayan architect Rafael Viñoly to replace a raft crossing over the lagoon on Ruta 10. Viñoly is responsible for Montevideo's small but perfectly-formed international airport and the pencil-thin New York skyscraper 432 Park Ave. The circular design forces drivers to slow down as they cross the water. There was a great deal of controversy regarding the building of the bridge which opened in 2016 as it will inevitably fast forward development of one of the last virgin areas of Maldonado but the reception has been generally positive, especially because the design welcomes walkers and fishing folk. Stop your car and take a walk around.

Laguna de Rocha See *Beaches, La Paloma*

Wine-tasting at Alto de la Ballena See *Wine Country, East coast* Thirty minutes drive

Pueblo Edén Surrounded by rolling hills, and just ten minutes north of the Alto de la Ballena winery, Pueblo Edén is a self-proclaimed slow town of less than a hundred inhabitants. The maximum speed limit is under 20 miles an hour and a sign at the entrance declares 'Only birds fly here'. If you want to see some of the interior of Uruguay, Pueblo Edén is a great choice. Stuff yourself on home-made pasta at the most rustic little eatery and have a coffee in the fanciest little cake shop you'll have the pleasure of running across in the Uruguayan countryside (see *Beaches, Punta Ballena, Where to eat*). It's an easy thirty minute drive along the glorious Ruta 12 which runs parallel to the Sierra de los Caracoles hill range.

Boutique olive oil production in Pueblo Edén Don't make the mistake of getting to Pueblo Edén and going no further. Fifteen minutes further along R12 becomes narrower and more winding. Lote 8 is an ultra chic olive oil producer perched on a hilltop deep in olive growing country with 360 degree views. There's a great little gift shop[5] which may solve some of your present needs. The views from Lote 8 and the well signed-posted drive up are as golden as their extra virgin.

What you should know

José Ignacio is still a semi-rural beach town despite its glamorous reputation. Hotel room televisions, high-tech gyms and decent Wi-Fi are not generally part of the package.

Restaurant reservations are essential. Expect to still have a long wait depending on the popularity of the restaurant.

Service is slow Expect to wait half an hour for your bill. Remember the slow pace is part of why you are in this part of the world.

Family-friendly You may be surprised that such exclusive beaches are children-friendly. Kids will be running among the supermodels and moguls. Even La Huella, Uruguay's most internationally famous restaurant, bills itself as a 'family-style restaurant'.

---

5   10% off gift shop purchases when you book your visit here www.guruguay.com/listings/lote-8

Getting around There are just two cabs in Jose Ignacio (two!) so have your own transportation or choose a hotel which offers bikes.

Nightlife Clubs are banned in Jose Ignacio. In high season head 12 miles (20 km) west to Montoya, Bikini and La Barra for multitudinous beach parties with music and DJs.

When to visit

Accommodation prices which are already high can quadruple during peak season and restaurants are heaving. Adjust your schedule to come October-mid December or March-April. Off season visit on weekends if you want to sample some of the best restaurants. They generally serve Friday dinner to Sunday lunchtime.

Where to stay

It was difficult to stay faithful to our criteria of only featuring hotels that stay open all year round on the peninsula. We were invited to check out the stunning Vik hotels of which there are several in Jose Ignacio and we were tempted. But no, our aim is to make Uruguay a year-round destination and we are staying true to ourselves.

Chacra El Silencio, R104 km 9

When Vicky and Jorge discovered a small piece of forested countryside that they loved horseriding to was up for sale they decided to build a small home there for themselves and their three sons. Two sons grew up and moved on, but Gonzalo became a chef (training at La Huella, naturally) and he opened a small restaurant on the property. Gonzalo is a specialist in bread baked in a clay oven. Jorge makes the cheeses. They have a kitchen garden and cook seasonally. Anything they don't grow is sourced locally and always organic. Customers—all attracted by word of mouth— couldn't believe that the family were not offering a place to stay given the chacra's very special solitude just minutes drive from trendy Playa Manantiales and Jose Ignacio. Now El Silencio is also a three room B&B (the master suite is 200ft square). Built for the outdoors, there are sofas and braziers on the porch and a small swimming pool. There are horses on the property and you can go riding there or on the beach in Jose Ignacio under the full moon. Write to Vicky at chacraelsilencio@gmail.com

Where to eat

There are a ton of very well-reviewed restaurants that open in the summertime but it's always impossible to know if they are going to open up again the next season. So faithful to our criteria, we are featuring three very different culinary options in Jose Ignacio which stay open all year round.

Parador La Huella

On a Sunday afternoon in May Jose Ignacio may be empty but La Huella will be packed. This ocean-front thatch-roofed beach-shack put Uruguayan cuisine on the map after a visit by Anthony Bourdin. La Huella (pronounced WAY-zzhah) has trained a generation of chefs and maître d's that ten years down the line are starting to have an impact on cuisine and culinary standards throughout Uruguay. Trained in La Huella has become a calling card. Specials include sirí crab and *pejerrey frito*, a crispy fried fish. Online booking is available 90 days in advance. Open daily in high season, off season Fridays-Sunday. Reserve at info@paradorlahuella.com

Carnicería Manolo

We're sending you to a butchers? Yes. This family-run business also runs a tasty take-away serving traditional Uruguayan food—*milanesas*, *empanadas* and cakes. You can also pick up local cheeses, fresh veggies and good wines. There are tables to eat outside and it's open all year round.

Panadería de la Mama

A bakery, coffee shop and deli with great prices. On the weekends there might be sushi. Open daily 9am-9pm, closed Tue-Wed off season.

How to get to Jose Ignacio

Ruta 10 km 183 Punta del Diablo (2 h), Montevideo (2 h 30 m) Punta del Este (40 m), Pueblo Edén (30 m)

Driving From Montevideo off season the most picturesque route is the coastal IB to Punta and then R10 around the peninsula of Punta del Este to Jose Ignacio (km 183). During high season avoid the centre of Punta del Este and take the R9, turning right at the signpost to Jose Ignacio (the road is called Camino Sainz Martinez). 40 km from Punta de Este and just 20 km from La Barra along the R10. From Punta del Diablo (110 km) take the R9 highway and make a left at km 161.

You cannot drive R10 between La Paloma and Jose Ignacio See *Beaches, La Paloma, How to get there*

Bus COT and COPSA from Montevideo to Jose Ignacio (apx. 3 hours). CODESA runs a local service between Jose Ignacio, La Barra and Punta del Este.

La Barra, Maldonado

La Barra is one of Punta del Este's trendiest neighbourhoods and one of the busiest during high season. Think the Hamptons meets Ibiza on spring break. La Barra was where artists from Punta escaped when Punta became too popular. Then the Argentinian glitterati bought houses there. La Barra is made up of lowrise apartments and houses set in a narrow forest—only ever minutes walk from the beach. The main street is a narrow strip lined with galleries, shabby-chic design stores, coffee shops and bars open till the early hours in summer and closed throughout the rest of the year, and *chivito* shops which open year round.

The beaches

All the action takes place to the east on three beaches—**Montoya** (the scene of surf events), **Bikini** (for obvious reasons) and **Manantiales**—where visiting Argentines and Brazilians seek to see and be seen. Paparazzi are on the hunt for models, soap opera stars and impresarios to populate the pages of *Hola! Argentina*. In high season DJs set up tiki torches around 4pm for chill-out sessions on the sand. **La Barra** beach at the mouth of the Maldonado river, which overlooks the wavy bridge to Punta, is a quieter beach with finer sands.

Things to do

Cross the wavy La Barra bridge Two picturesque bridges with gentle roller-coaster curves connect La Barra to Punta del Este over the river Maldonado. Previous bridges had been washed away when Leonel Viera, a Uruguayan builder with no academic qualifications, built the first of the two bridges in 1965. So enchanted was Chilean poet Pablo Neruda by its feminine design that he composed an ode to the bridge. A second identical bridge was built in 1998 to take pressure off the original. The official name of the bridge is the Leonel Viera La Barra Bridge but everyone calls it the Wavy Bridge (*puente ondulante* in Spanish).

Atchugarry Sculpture Park Pablo Atchugarry is one of Uruguay's leading sculptors based half of the year in Italy and the other half in Punta del Este. His foundation and thirty-hectare (74-acre) sculpture park in the countryside a few minutes drive from the La Barra offers exhibitions and concerts in the summertime and an annual exhibition of a major artist or collection (such as František Kupka and Le Corbusier). Ruta 104 km 4.5 from El Chorro. Open daily Jan-Feb 10am-9pm Mar-Dec Tue-Sat 9am-6pm

Party houses (*fiestas en las casitas*) Rather than open a club in recent years the trend has been for promoters to rent a house for the summer, fix it up as a bar and throw open the doors to the public.

Inland La Barra Bike Tour This tour leaves from the Wavy Bridge in La Barra or Punta del Este. Your destination is one of Latin America's top hotels by way of a boutique winery. The riding includes an initial gentle slope uphill (great free-wheeling back down). Email alicia@biketoursuruguay.com

Punta Birdwatching See *Beaches, Punta del Este, Things to Do*

Wine-tasting at Alto de la Ballena See *Wine Country, East coast*

Slow town Pueblo Edén See *Beaches, Jose Ignacio, Things to do*

What you should know

Accommodation prices soar The lowrises and houses cannot accommodate the number of people interested in staying in La Barra in high season. Book well in advance and read amenity details and reviewers comments carefully.

Arriving by car It's a must to have your own transport in La Barra. Taxis from Punta del Este airport are extremely expensive and local buses heaving with teenagers.

When to visit

Partiers and twenty-somethings will love high season. The rest of the year La Barra virtually closes down and becomes as solitary and peaceful as its neighbours.

Where to stay

Kalá Boutique Hotel, La Barra

This Mykonos-inspired hotel is set on a gentle hill a six-minute walk from Playa Montoya. Their fourteen rooms are large and comfortable with king size beds and balconies or terraces looking out onto the turquoise pool. There are a number of lounge areas for relaxing and contemplating the hummingbirds besides a solarium, a bar, an open air area for yoga and a sauna. Owner Pablo goes out of his way to make guests feel special. Remarkably Kalá has held on to the same staff including Virginia in reception since they opened seven years ago—a feat of team management regrettably infrequent on the Uruguayan coast. Kalá is a great place for honeymooners and couples. Breakfast includes home-made bread and cakes, eggs cooked to order and fresh fruit. During high season they also offer a simple lunch service of chunky sandwiches and salads for guests only. There is parking on site and bikes for getting around locally. Write to Pablo at info@kalahotel.com or visit www.kalahotel.com

Where to eat

El Chancho y La Coneja

Hidden amidst eucalyptus trees and rosemary bushes, just off from the wavy bridge, this rustic family restaurant run by him, the Pig (Chancho) and her, the Rabbit (when I asked a local what their real names were, she said to me she had no idea and that she only knew them by their nicknames) is infamous for their delicious food, huge portions, veggie options and friendliest staff. Their cheesecake (*tarta de ricota batida con lemoncello*) with home-made strawberry topping is a classic. Open high season daily for dinner, lunch on weekends; low season Fri-Sat dinner, Sat-Sun lunch

Pizzeria La Fusa

This little pizza place set several blocks back from the main street in La Barra was recommended by the slow food folks at El Silencio for their thin-crust pizzas, fresh ingredients and low prices. Specialities include *fainá*, a thick baked chickpea pancake. Open high season daily 9pm-1am; low season daily 8-11.30pm closed Mondays

How to get to La Barra

R10 km 159 Punta del Este (15 m), Jose Ignacio (25 m), Montevideo (2 h 15 m)

Driving See *Punta del Este*. La Barra is just 10-15 minutes drive on from Punta del Este.

Bus Even though it is close to Punta, there is limited public transport to La Barra. From Montevideo, just a few buses (COT and COPSA) leave per day (2h 40m) to 'Barra de Maldonado'. Buses (Micro Ltda) depart from the terminal in Punta del Este every hour from 10am-6pm and every half an hour during the summertime. Note they are generally too crowded to carry luggage. The 3A (CODESA) stops at the Punta del Este shopping centre and goes to La Barra.

Punta del Este, Maldonado

Punta del Este or Punta as it's colloquially known is the most famous beach resort in southern South America. Less than ten thousand people live there year round, a number which explodes to 300,000 in summer. Over 150 years ago, Punta and its surroundings were miles and miles of sand and dunes. Legend has it that the first settler used camels as work animals. Seeing how virgin and beautiful the area was, the first holiday homes were built at the turn of the twentieth century and local and Argentinian developers started to promote the Punta del Este as it became officially known in 1907. That same year, a company with the novel name of Snowball chartered steamboats from Montevideo and Buenos Aires to bring well-off holidaymakers to sample 'paradise', buy land and spread the word that Punta was where it was at.

The coastal promenade or rambla was built in 1911 and hotels, followed by casinos and nightclubs. With the arrival of the railroad in the 1930s Punta was just three hours from Montevideo. In the 1950s a very few highrises started to appear though Punta's reputation as a luxury glamour resort was protected by urban planners following guidelines by Spanish architect Bonet. Bonet prioritised the beach and the woods, large plots, meandering streets (unusual in this part of the world where streets are usually grid-aligned) and carefully separating residential areas from commercial ones.

This paradise attracted artists and creative types. The first Punta international film festival, today Latin America's oldest film festival, premièred in 1951. With over than sixty galleries, Punta is still a hub for nowadays well-off artists. From the 80s Punta saw an explosion of highrise apartment buildings especially along the Playa Mansa. If you visit Punta del Este off season, you will be amazed to see hundreds of tower blocks in virtual complete darkness. The vast majority are owned by Argentinians as investments—when you live in an unstable economy, if you have the means you sink them into bricks-and-mortar.

The Peninsula is packed with the most emblematic of Punta—the famous 'hand' sculpture rising from the sand and the marina where millionaires moor their yachts. During summer, Punta del Este attracts Argentines and Brazilians looking to see and be seen and if they are not in La Barra they are cruising up and down the peninsula. Be prepared for bumper-to-bumper traffic along the principal high streets, Gorlero Avenue and Calle 20, known as Fashion Road. Shops range from typical tourist tat to the most exclusive designers.

Punta del Este has two long **beaches**—the **Brava** and the **Mansa**—both lined with highrises. Playa Brava is to the east and as its name suggests the waves are rougher and it's less sheltered. The Mansa to the west is more protected. The peninsula has a couple of small rocky beach coves. Local legend has it that one, the English Beach (Playa de Los Ingleses) was named after expats who would picnic complete with tea-set.

Palatial leafy neighbourhoods like Parque del Golf are the exclusive 'old money' *barrios*—a world away from the throngs on Gorlero. The sumptuous residences set in pine groves date from the first decades of Punta. These houses have large grounds without fences, illustrating how safe the city is.

Punta del Este is the **birthplace of Uruguay's most famous sandwich, the Chivito** created in 1944. Antonio Carbonaro ran a bar on the peninsula on the corner of Calles 31 and 32. One day a customer from the mountain area of Argentina was on her way back home and wanted to order something quick. She asked for baby goat (*chivito*). The kitchen was closed but Antonio was eager to please. He buttered a bread roll and made a sandwich with a slice of ham on a quarter-pound sliver of steak. The lady loved it and he baptised the sandwich a *chivito*. Carbonaro went on to sell a thousand *chivitos* a day. Over time more ingredients were added including cheese, tomato, lettuce, ham, bacon, egg and olives, making the *chivito* which you'll inevitably find in any Uruguayan restaurant anywhere in the world.

Things to do

Old Punta and the port Have a wander around the old part of Peninsula above the port—it's a very different Punta from the highrise-lined coast. By old I mean solid inter-war houses and some lowrise apartments, nothing colonial. The port and marina are also charming with a yacht club and several restaurants. At the marina watch the local fishermen cleaning their catch and tossing the left-overs to the huge seals basking next to the yachts. In the evenings, Moby Dick, a pub/club open all year round just opposite the port is frequented by singles over thirty. A number of craft beer gardens have opened in the area—start out at Capi Bar and get your bearings from there.

Visit the Hand Few people leave Punta del Este without taking a photo of themselves posing next to the giant fingers emerging from the sand at Parada 1 on Playa Brava. The sculpture *Man Emerging into Life* by Chilean Mario Irarrázabal was created in 1982.

Punta bike tours After a family crisis, bike enthusiast Alicia Barbitta decided to make some serious life changes. She moved to Punta from Montevideo and now leads classic bike tours across Uruguay. Her most popular tour is the Punta Peninsula tour which takes you around the peninsula on the promenade with fantastic views of the ocean. Her Mystical Punta tour bikes though some of the city's oldest neighbourhoods and includes a testing ground where Marconi, the inventor of the telegraph who lived in Punta 1910-11, made the first transatlantic radio contact to Europe. Contact Alicia for information about tours to La Barra and Punta Ballena and bespoke tours to discover more of Uruguay's quiet beauty by bike. Alicia speaks great English and provides the type of historical and social detail that will make your tour really informative. Contact alicia@biketoursuruguay.com

Museo Ralli A collection of Latin American bronze sculptures and a varied collection of contemporary Latin American art, complemented by European works by artists of the stature of Dali. In the Beverly Hills neighbourhood in a garden setting, entry is free.

Punta Salinas and the Battle of the River Plate At the far end of the peninsula lies Punta Salinas, where the River Plate officially ends and the Atlantic Ocean begins. It's the southernmost point of Uruguay. From this point locals watched World War II history in the making as the British Royal Navy cruisers Ajax, Exeter and Achilles fought the Graf Spee in the Battle of the River Plate in 1939. The Ajax's anchor lies in the Plaza Gran Bretaña.

Punta Birdwatching Gonzalo Millacet leads tours through the Parque Indigena, a national park on the Maldonado river remarkably just ten minutes outside the city centre. The park has been designated an important bird and biodiversity area by Birdlife International. Two hundred and thirty species have been registered there, including flamingos. The tour lasts two hours and you'll see 30-40 species. Gonzalo provides a checklist in English and binoculars. Enthusiasts should ask about an all-day tour to Jose Ignacio and the Laguna Garzón. 25 USD. Email info@birdwatchingtours.uy

Whale-watching The most common view points are on the Mansa beach between *Paradas* 23 and 40 and Punta Salinas.

Wine-tasting at Alto de la Ballena See *Wine Country, East coast*

Slow town Pueblo Edén See *Beaches, Jose Ignacio, Things to do*

Cabo Polonio nature tour If you only have a day to visit Rocha, this is a great full-day option. Your group will be picked up in or around Punta, drive 2.5 hours and take the exhilarating truck ride through the dunes to Cabo. Your guide Juan Pablo Millacet speaks great English and has fifteen years experience in Cabo. You'll visit the seal colony, there's time for lunch (he has the best tips of where to eat) and then an hour long walk to the dunes to see Darwin's Toad and other native species. Email info@cabopolonioecotours.com

What you should know

In summer, is Punta really part of Uruguay? Argentinians and Brazilians go crazy for Punta. When I lived in Argentina years ago the endless TV coverage of the Punta beach scene invariably focused on the *cola-less*, a tiny g-string, seemingly obligatory beach wear for any female celeb or wannabe. *Cola* is Spanish for buttocks. The colas and Punta were so ubiquitous, I actually thought Punta was part of Argentina until I looked on a map. Nothing has changed. Just look at any Argentinian website catering to "luxury travel in Argentina at its very finest" and Punta is there—without a single mention of it being in Uruguay. We can conclude that in summer, Punta is no longer truely part of Uruguay. I suspect most Uruguayans would agree.

Getting around – the Paradas There is no street numbering on the rambla in Punta del Este. 'Paradas' or numbered signposts on the oceanfront are used instead. Numbering starts from the peninsula and head west along the Mansa beach and north along the Brava beach. So there's a Parada 1 on the Mansa and a different Parada 1 on the Brava. If someone gives you an address using a Parada, make sure you know which beach they are referring to.

If you want to explore you'll need a car Punta is a city and distances are significant. Taxis are expensive—perhaps because they are all Mercedes! Local buses are infrequent. The Easy Taxi app was allowed into the taxi market in 2017 but is currently limited to the city of Punta del Este and does not include airport rides. These restrictions may be relaxed in the future.

When to visit

Punta is heaving with tourists from Christmas Eve to the end of February. If you love crowds and nightlife then you should definitely check out high season Punta. If you don't, you can totally give it a miss without a second thought. Off season Punta has a charm of its own.

Where to stay

I recommend staying in a hotel to get the full Punta glamour experience.

L'Auberge

Any Uruguayan will tell you that the best hotel in Punta del Este is L'Auberge. The emblematic tower of the Edwardian-style five-star hotel was the first building in what would become Punta's most elegant neighbourhood, Parque del Golf. The tower originally provided water to the surrounding residences, all sumptuous mansions. In 1981, the tower was remodelled into small but original guestrooms. The other 21 guestrooms are large suites, impeccably decorated and all with garden views. The tearoom is famous for its Belgian waffles, the original owners being Belgians who brought the waffle irons that are still used every afternoon to Uruguay. The outdoor swimming pool is beautifully maintained all year round. Service is delightful, nothing is too much. A stay at L'Auberge is your opportunity to step back into the gracious origins of Punta. No wonder their guests come back year after year. Write to Ignacio at lauberge@laubergehotel.com or visit www.laubergehotel.com $$$$-$$$$$

The Grand Hotel

If L'Auberge is Old Punta, The Grand Hotel is New Punta. With 136 rooms right on the Playa Brava, it's the city's second largest hotel with a sleek modern glass-and-metal design, colourful pop-chic décor and electro-pop mood music. I was intrigued because for a large hotel it was garnering really great guest reviews . All ocean-front rooms have floor to ceiling sea views. The giant beds with their Italian bedding and the most comfortable pillows ever face the ocean. There are indoor, outdoor and Turkish-style pools and unexpected touches like a 50-seater cinema showing movies twice a day and welcome drinks on Friday evenings with the staff. The buffet breakfast was exceptional with a full English on request and champagne! The only issue is a lack of English speaking staff but they make up for it with their can-do attitude and warmth. The Grand is beach-front but as building is restricted on the coast line you have to cross a main road to reach the beach. Email info@puntagrand.com www.puntagrand.com $$$$

Where to eat

481 Gourmet, Punta del Este

Tucked down a commercial side-street a couple of blocks from Punta's main shopping centre, this 'meat boutique' is a fantastic discovery. From the antipasto (buffalo cheese, arugula, almonds), to the perfectly cooked rack of lamb and crispy home-made fries, every ingredient was wonderfully fresh and so delicious. The waiters and the grill chef really know their meat and they love to talk cuts. **Cuts in Uruguay are very different from what you have at home so be adventurous**. Tell your waiter the texture you like and go for a cut you would never usually be able to try. If money is no object, try their Wagyu, ultra-premium Uruguay-raised Japanese beef. A word of warning. You are visiting a *boutique de carnes*. An entire wall of the restaurant is lined with displays of vacuum-packed prime beef. There is outside seating though the location is not very attractive. But you are here for the ultimate Uruguayan carnivore experience, which is top class without breaking the bank. Open high season daily noon-4pm and 6-11pm; off season Thu-Sun 8pm-midnight, Fri-Sat and holidays noon-4pm. Email Matias at parrilla481gourmet@gmail.com

Capi Bar, Peninsula, Punta del Este

Capi Bar was the first craft beer bar to open in Punta. Owner, chef and keen surfer, Diego Tarallo, was captain of his childhood football team hence the nickname, Capi. He makes his own brews sold in the bar together with over forty draft and bottled beers from all over Uruguay. The restaurant part of Capi has taken them to No 1 in TripAdvisor in Punta. They serve *ceviche*, grilled salmon, a seafood grill for two and home-made hamburgers, all at reasonable prices, especially for Punta. Look out for Capi Bar in La Barra in high season. Open daily 1pm-3am info@capibar.com.uy

Macachín, Maldonado

Perhaps this is the best restaurant in the whole of Uruguay. That's certainly what Uruguay and Argentina's top chefs particularly in the slow food community think. Macachín is a tiny 18-seater restaurant down an unassuming side-street in the decidedly non-touristy city of Maldonado, fifteen minutes from Punta. Fronted by cook (he dislikes the term chef) and ex-motorbike mechanic Adrian Orio, who cooks "creative Uruguayan cuisine", ingredients are local, organic, foraged or home-grown. A main dish was *burriqueta* with a puree of Jerusalem artichoke in a lemon and *catay* sauce. I'd never seen these ingredients on a menu in Uruguay before. *Burriqueta* is a fish prized by amateurs, unheard of at a fishmongers. *Catay*, spicy like watercress, grows wild in marshes. With its front patio lined with wooden boxes of herbs and flowers (Adrian's partner Mariela went out to pick some with tweezers for our dessert) you could be in a French country bistro. Adrian prioritises flavour over everything else. The dish may look amazing but it also has to taste amazing. Portions are ample and prices are unbelievable. A three-course meal plus a drink and appetizers costs under 1000 pesos. You must not miss this. Open Tue-Sat 8.30pm-midnight, Sun 12.30 noon-4pm (reservations only). Reservations at macachinmaldonado@gmail.com

Juana V See *Beaches, Punta Ballena, Where to Eat*

How to get to Punta del Este

IB km 134 Montevideo (2 h), Punta del Diablo (2 h 30 m), Jose Ignacio (40 m)

Driving From Montevideo (140 km) just over two hours' very easy drive along the IB and then the coastal rambla. If you are staying on Playa Brava or in La Barra, a short-cut to avoid the peninsula is to turn left at Parada 4 (Mansa) onto Av Chiverta, rejoining the rambla on Playa Brava. From Carrasco International Airport 25 km east of Montevideo, the drive is 115 km along the IB and takes just under two hours. 40 minutes from Jose Ignacio on R10.

From Punta del Este airport Two daily flights land from Buenos Aires and Brazil, with additional flights in high season. Buses (COPSA and COT) connect to the city. At the time of writing, transport apps were banned from serving the airport. See *Practical Tips, Getting to Uruguay, Airports*

From Brazil Buses (TTL and EGA) stop in Punta del Este on their way to Montevideo.

Bus COPSA and COT travel every hour from Montevideo and Carrasco International Airport. There are reasonable connections with other parts of Uruguay.

Punta Ballena & Piriapolis, Maldonado

Punta Ballena is a ocean-side neighbourhood and the name given to a six-mile area encompassing the beaches that line the bay of Portezuelo. Even though it's just a twenty-minute drive from Punta del Este the vibe changes—the resorts nestle in peaceful green forests though in high season there's some partying and nightlife. Punta Ballena itself is a rocky peninsula where the sierra plunges into the ocean. The area was settled by Lussich, a shipping magnate who built himself a mansion on the point with an immaculate view over the bay. The point was so exposed to the Atlantic winds that his wife issued an ultimatum—do something about the wind or she'd blow out taking the family with her. In response, he planted hundreds of thousands of trees and what would become the second largest arboretum in South America. Years later Uruguayan abstract artist Carlos Páez Vilaró bought a large plot on the peninsula—he claimed that at the time a square foot of the land cost the price of a packet of cigarettes—and started building his now world-famous Casapueblo home and atelier.

The beaches

Chihuahua was Uruguay's first official nudist beach designated back in the 1960s. As usual Uruguay was at the vanguard—the first ever nudist beach had only been declared a decade earlier in France. During the summer up to three thousand people visit each day. Nudity is optional. Today Chihuahua is mostly known as a gay beach[6].

---

6   Uruguay is considered the most gay friendly country in South America www.guruguay.com/uruguay-gay-friendly

The forest that would become **Ocean Park** was named by Argentine investors. Of course. Argentines just love to adopt English or European place names. Hence the dirt roads in the middle of the forest are baptised Biarritz, Palm Beach, etc. The investors opened an office in downtown Buenos Aires in the 1960s to great fanfare and sold most of the lots. But their plan to create an exclusive private neighbourhood fell apart as very few of the buyers actually got round to building houses. Even today the modern and minimalist beach homes, elegantly set amongst quiet pine and eucalyptus forests, are very few.

I just have to mention the unfortunately named beach, Tio Tom (Uncle Tom). Us English readers may cringe, but I can assure you that noone here does. The owner of the original Uncle Tom's Cabins (yes, really) built in the early 1970s owned a bus company and doubtless cared not one hoot about the literature or racial politics of the USA. Still, go stay in Ocean Park anyway.

Piriapolis and Punta Colorada

Less than half an hour's drive from Punta Ballena lies **Piriapolis**, a classic Uruguayan beach resort with a long promenade and a 1950s air. The beach, which is mainly frequented by Uruguayan families, is wide and flat and as the water is extremely calm and shallow it's ideal for small children. The Hotel Argentino, an art-Deco gem, dominates the rambla. Built in the 1920s it was South America's largest and most glamorous resort. Today it is still a Piriapolis icon though unfortunately a little run-down. The award-winning Uruguayan film *Whisky* was filmed there. Take the chairlift up the San Antonio Hill. The view of the bay is stunning. The chairlift looks precarious but I've braved it myself and in almost two decades living in Uruguay have never heard of an accident! Five kilometres east of Piriapolis lies **Punta Colorada**, a spectacular oceanic beach.

Things to do

Casapueblo Carlos Páez Vilaró (1923-2014), Uruguayan abstract artist, sculptor and friend to Pablo Picasso and Brigitte Bardot, purchased the virgin Punta Ballena in 1958. Initially he built himself a small summer house on the side of the cliff. Then as he needed more space, or friends came to stay, he built an extension. Eventually Casapueblo became a breathtaking thirteen-storey white-washed citadel staggered down the side of the peninsula. Páez Vilaró called it a habitable sculpture made in the style of the *hornero*, a native bird which builds cave-like nests from mud. Now open to the public, you can visit the gallery and café and enjoy a marvellous view over the Atlantic. The Sun Ceremony, an audio recording of the artist bidding the sun farewell, plays every day on the terrace and is a Punta classic. There is an entrance fee. Exit IB at km 119.5 and follow the signs about a mile towards the water. Open daily 10am till sundown

Arboretum Lussich This park is the considered the most important forest reserve in South America and the seventh in the world. Its 450 acres include 370 types of exotic tree and sixty native to Uruguay. Unfortunately invading species have taken over so as a botanical initiative it leaves much to be desired. As an afternoon walk it's highly recommendable. The views as far as Piriapolis are marvellous, especially at sunset. As are the clusters of humming birds and huge birds of prey sailing just overhead. It's easy walking from one end of the park to the other—you can do it in half an hour if you are pushed for time, but I would suggest taking a leisurely three hours and a picnic. Turn off IB at km 119 and 500m up the hill. Open daily 10am-5.30pm

Punta Ballena Bike tour This bike tour is a great way of checking out Casapueblo, the Arboretum and finding out more about Punta del Este and Punta Ballena from a local English-speaking guide who is also a bit of a history buff. If your ride coincides with sundown, join the Sun Ceremony at Casapueblo. Start the tour from Punta or Punta Ballena. Email alicia@biketoursuruguay.com

Wildlife watching Punta Ballena means Whale Point. You can whale-watch from the beach and from the top of the Punta Ballena peninsula. Birdwatchers will find the river area around the Potrero river which divides Chihuahua from Ocean Park attractive.

Fishing, sandboarding and golf The beaches and rivers of Punta Ballena are great fishing spots. There are reports of 8kg *lenguado* (sole or flounder) being landed from the Arroyo Potrero. The dunes around the *arroyo* are great sandboarding fun for children. Sandboards are for sale on the side of the IB directly after the first toll booths leaving Montevideo. If you are going to a dune area with kids it's a worthwhile investment.

Nightlife During high season, Resto Bar Mulata is the centre of nightlife in Chihuahua. There's dancing, well-known DJs and a relaxed, friendly crowd of all diversities.

Day trip to Piriapolis This circuit takes you along the highway to one of Uruguay's oldest resorts, Solis, along a scenic coastal road to Piriapolis and then back to Punta along the highway by a different scenic route. Start by driving along the IB toward Montevideo. Take the exit to Balneario Solis (km 83). This scenic coastal road to Piriapolis passes several lovely little beach towns. After visiting Piriapolis, follow the coastal road east past the port. Take time to visit the beaches at Punta Colorada—which has some nice little eateries in high season—and Punta Negra. To return to Punta del Este, continue along the coastal road (called Americas Unidas from Punta Colorada) which will turn inland. The road will seem to be going nowhere. Don't worry, in 4-5 km you will reach the IB. Turn right onto it taking care of oncoming traffic.

Wine-tasting at Alto de la Ballena See *Wine Country, East coast*

Visit Pueblo Edén See *Beaches, Jose Ignacio, Things to do*

What you should know

Consider having a car if you stay in Punta Ballena You can reach the area by bus—you will get dropped off on the highway and will generally not have more than a 10-15 minute walk to your accommodation but public transport is infrequent.

When to visit

You can visit all year round. It's happening in the summer but not over the top. A number of small supermarkets open all year round.

Where to stay

We would have loved to recommend Casapueblo but varying reviews and their lack of response to our attempts to reach them meant that we were not able to check it out for ourselves. But we did find this lovely little budget place in the woods.

Cabañas del Potrero, Ocean Park

The Ocean Park effect. Families arrive revved up with plans of where to go and what to see. A few hours later they're dozing on their cabin deck, voices hushed, soaking in the forest. These six cabañas are beautifully-maintained and designed with privacy in mind. The owners Ana Ines and Ruben have planted hedges and erected wooden fences to cordon off the small swimming pool, the two Uruguay-style barbecue grills with tables and benches and each cabin from each other. A secret short-cut through the trees means you are down at the beach within two minutes. Each cabin has its own ingeniously-equipped kitchen. Breakfast supplies (wonderbread but a nice selection of jams and *dulce de leche* and ample milk and juice) arrive the evening before so you can serve yourself when you like. There's daily maid service. Each cabin has a charcoal grill. Bikes, beach chairs, towels and sun umbrellas are free to use. You can hear the low hum of the nearby highway but Potrero has really achieved a level of tranquillity that is very special. This is budget accommodation at its local best. IB km 111. Their small green signs pop up on every corner making arrival really easy. Write to Ana Ines at info@cabaniasdelpotrero.com or visit www.cabaniasdelpotrero.com $$

Where to eat

There are no recommended restaurants open all year round but just out on the highway is the food truck with the mostest. And several *incredible* restaurants 15-20 minutes drive away.

El Lobo Suelto, Punta Ballena

By the side of the highway, Monica and co. go the extra mile with their traditional Uruguayan fast food. They serve *chivitos*, home-made hamburgers and fish of the day along with organic salads and pastas (like mushroom and roast veggie lasagna. Juana V recommends their canelones). The winter menu includes Uruguayan hotpot classics like lentil stew (*cazuela de lentejas*) and Brazilian black bean f*eijoada*. During summer they serve fruit juices and smoothies. IB km 118 opposite the ANCAP gas station. Open daily noon-midnight, low season Tue-Sat 11am-4.30pm

Macachín, Maldonado See *Punta del Este* 15 minutes drive, don't miss it

Juana V, Camino a la Capilla de la Asuncion

After specialising in charcuterie in Paris, French chef Laurence Lamare acquired Juana V, a former tea room in the panoramic Sierra de la Ballena just outside of Punta to set up what she calls a *pulpería*—or a general store. She sells her own cured and aged meats and sausages, as well as crusty baguettes. Out back is a restaurant. Laurence cooks what is in season in their certified organic kitchen garden. A typical meal includes appetizers, salad from the garden, main course, dessert (maybe her famous crepes) and coffee all for 1000 pesos. Children half price. There's also all-you-can-eat parrilla with Juana V's own aged meats. Go with time to spend the entire afternoon on the outdoor deck warmed by the afternoon sun. Open Fri-Sun 12-7pm. Reservations are essential. Email laurencelamare@hotmail.com (20 minute drive)

La Posta de Vaimaca, Pueblo Edén

This ramshackle cabin famous for its roasted lamb and home-made pasta is run by a local couple who fell in love with slow town Pueblo Edén in the 90s. They grow and rear just about every ingredient on the menu. Favourites are roasted lamb and rabbit in mushroom sauce. For vegetarians and vegans there are home-made pasta dishes with a choice of sauce. Reservations are essential by phone +598 98 025049 or Facebook message. They are quick to answer (in Spanish). Open daily 12.30-4pm closed Mondays (30 minute drive)

La Casita del Chocolate, Pueblo Edén

The Little House of Chocolate is an obligatory stop for good coffee and home-made desserts and chocolate in the centre of Pueblo Edén, a short stroll from Vaimaca. As well as desserts, the Casita sells sandwiches, home-made bread and ice-cream. Open daily noon-8pm closed Tuesday and Wednesdays

How to get to Punta Ballena

Punta del Este Airport **IB km 113** Ocean Park **IB km 111** Punta Ballena **IB km 119.5**

Driving From Montevideo apx. 120 km along the IB (2 h). It is very simple to get to any of the beaches coming from the west as they all lie directly south of the IB highway. You just need to know the km marker number. Beach names are clearly signposted. Coming from Punta de Este 13 km along the IB (10 m), take care when exiting as you will be crossing the highway.

Punta del Este airport is just two kilometres from Ocean Park along the IB.

Bus From Montevideo buses (COT and COPSA) pick up and drop off passengers at exits to the beaches on the IB highway. Request a ticket to your desired beach and make sure the driver knows where you need to descend, though watch the km markers too just in case. From Montevideo, buses to Piriapolis are frequent (2 h). Between Punta and Piriapolis, take the CODESA number 8 bus via Punta Colorada which runs several times a day. Buses (CODESA and Maldonado Turismo) run along the coast between Punta Ballena, Punta del Este, La Barra, Manantiales and Jose Ignacio.

Whale-watching

Between July and November the southern right whale visits the coastline of Maldonado and Rocha to breed in the warmer waters. The amazing thing about watching whales in Uruguay is that you don't need to hire a boat or contract an expensive trip. You can actually watch whales right from the beach. Incredibly the whales are just feet from you and binoculars will make the experience even better.

How come it's possible to see whales from the beach? Between Punta del Diablo and Piriapolis, the water close to the coast is very deep, making it an ideal play and breeding ground for these huge beasties as they migrate between Argentina and Brazil. Think of Uruguay as a kind of gigantic whale spa.

Sighting a whale is not guaranteed. But there's a citizen watch network on Facebook which makes it much more likely. The members of the *Red de Avistaje de Ballena Franca y Delfines*[7] (South Right Whale and Dolphin watch network) are people living locally who post their sightings of whales and other sea mammals as they happen. As they share time of sighting, location and photos, it's a unique, real-time resource. The group is in Spanish but just switch on 'translate'. Keep checking the page during your visit and be ready to jump in your car.

How to spot whales

The best times to observe are the early hours of the morning and late in the day, when the waters are calm. Look out for:

- flocks of gulls circling – they hover above submerged whales
- churning water
- spray – the whale shooting water through its blow hole, don't expect it to necessarily form a 'V' shape
- glistening in the water – the reflection on the whale's back.

Some recommended viewing points

- Punta Colorada and Punta Negra (east of Piriapolis)
- Punta del Este between Paradas 23 and 40 and Punta Salinas on the peninsula
- La Paloma
- La Pedrera
- Playa Grande, Punta del Diablo.

The official whale season is between July and November however some years they have arrived in early June.

---

7   www.facebook.com/groups/reddeavistaje

Shipwreck spotting

The Uruguayan coast is treacherous. Centuries ago, ships arriving from the Atlantic suddenly found themselves encountering a rocky coastline with capes and islands, and hidden sandbanks. The very first expedition party from Europe, led by Juan Diaz de Solis who was following the eastern coast of South America southward as far as he could, reached the mouth of the River Plate in 1516 and named it Río de la Plata. But not before one of his expedition ships ran aground. As time passed sailors identified the different capes by their shapes or by the wildlife that they saw from their boats. Thus naming Castillos (Castles), Aguas Dulces (Sweet Waters), La Paloma (The Dove), Isla de los Lobos (Sealion Island), Punta del Este (Eastern Point) and Punta Ballena (Whale Point).

In the period immediately prior to the construction of the first lighthouses, Uruguay as a nation was in a period of growing pains. The young republic independent in the 1830s faced institutional crises and uprisings. Then in 1868 a terrible maritime tragedy shook the country. A passenger ship the Lise Amelie carrying hundreds of Scottish immigrants smashed on to the coast of Rocha, leaving not one survivor.

Such was the horror that disputing factions came together to pass a law to build the lighthouse where La Paloma is located today and the 1870s saw a period of lighthouse-building all along the coast. Sadly despite the lighthouses, casualties were expected. The specifications for the lighthouse in La Paloma included a room "especially destined for castaways and equipped with inclined beds, first aid kit and other equipment to provide the first aid to the wretches that the lighthouse will have undoubtedly warned, but not preserved from the caprice of the sea". All the lighthouses remain active today.

Shipwreck spotting

As you walk along any beach, chances are you'll run into the remains of ships, their skeletons emerging from the sea or resting on the sand. Here are some locations to visit on your travels. Note the nature of shipwrecks mean that they may not be visible or may have been washed away.

Sand bar at Laguna Garzón - the ship's boiler of an unknown ship
Las Garzas – at exceptionally low tide the remains of a French vessel the Poitou
Playa Corumba, La Paloma – the ship's boiler of a Brazilian boat which ran the Montevideo-Rio de Janeiro line sunk in 1874
Playa del Barco, La Pedrera – the remains of the Taiwanese tuna fishing boat the Cathay VIII which ran aground in the 1970s. The crew disembarked and were provided for by the townspeople
Aguas Dulces – Junior wrecked in 1869 is occasionally visible in the water and the Gainford a British steamship sunk in 1884
La Esmeralda – a cargo ship Cocal ran aground in 1969
La Coronilla – the steamship Porteña ran aground in 1873

Atlantida & the Costa de Oro, Canelones

A series of twenty-six fine white sandy beaches lined with woodland and small settlements of permanent and holiday residences stretch for thirty miles along Uruguay's Costa de Oro—the Gold Coast. The sands are beautifully powdery thanks to this being the River Plate estuary.

Historically the Costa de Oro was mainly dune and marshes, ignored because of its aridity. Then around 1870, wealthy families started to arrive to escape the heat of summer in Montevideo. Dragging their goods including chickens and milk cows across the dunes, they would set up camp for three months at a time. To halt the movement of the dunes the first pine trees were brought over from Spain and Portugal in 1908. Pines, eucalyptus and acacias are still planted today for the same purpose.

The Costa de Oro is the bastion of middle class Uruguayans and many have holiday homes here given it's an hour or so from the capital. So you're more likely to be surrounded by Uruguayan holiday-makers than by other nationalities. The Costa de Oro is a great base for travellers looking to live like a local in a beach environment.

The beaches

The beaches lie between the River Pando to the west and the River Solis to the east. The first beaches from **Neptunia** to **Mar India** are home to Uruguayans living there full-time. Residences range from comfortable middle-class chalets to run-down shacks.

The lovely **Fortín de Santa Rosa** (km 41.5) is the first beach where you start to feel that this is a primarily holiday community. The area was forested in the 1930s and the locals pride themselves on the preservation of the local flora (there's even a little community-managed nature reserve). Santa Rosa is very secluded. In winter it's a great place to fish. Plan to do lots of long walks along the beach to neighbouring settlements. Atlantida is a 40-50 minute walk. Under ten miles from the international airport, Santa Rosa is perfect for starting or ending your trip and to experience Uruguay's beaches with absolutely minimal travel.

Atlantida (km 45) is thirty minutes drive from the outskirts of Montevideo and is one of the most populated towns on the Costa de Oro with a stable population of about 6,000 including a growing community of North American and European expats. It has two long pine-tree lined beaches, the Mansa which stretches down to Villa Argentina and the infamous Eagle head, and the Brava to the east. On the rambla there are a number of picturesque Elizabethan-style houses including one where the Chilean poet Pablo Neruda used to meet his lover. The Eagle and the art-Deco Planet on the rambla (once one of Uruguay's smartest hotels, now apartments) were built by an Italian immigrant who ran a casino in the 1950s , where the likes of Julio Iglesias played and the Miss Uruguay pageant was held. Atlantida has a very complete town centre with a number of supermarkets including a hypermarket out by the highway. There is some nightlife on weekends and holidays. Most social interaction takes place on the rambla with groups hanging out till the very early hours of the morning.

Leaving Atlantida, the two biggest beach communities before the Solis Chico river are **Las Toscas** (km 47) and **Parque del Plata** (km 49). The beaches are wilder and dotted with people fishing and the occasional surfer. Vacation rentals here are of a higher category in general compared to beaches closer to Montevideo. From the beach the coastal road is hidden from sight by dunes and pine trees. Both settlements are attracting permanent residents (including many from overseas). The last census put Parque del Plata's population at almost 8,000 so there is more and more year-round infrastructure.

La Floresta (km 54) took its name from the forestry company that planted a million trees on the dunes in the early 1900s. Like Atlantida it's a very established town by Uruguayan beach standards with people owning their holiday homes there for generations. The art-Deco ex-hotel on the coast built in 1915 was the tallest building on the entire coast and boasted a casino and a cinema. In summer residents promote family-friendly activities like the Noche Blanca, or White Night, a cultural event adopted from France for the centenary of the town in 2009 which takes place on the Friday or Saturday closest to the first full moon of December.

Things to do

Hang out on the rambla Uruguayans of all ages hang out on the rambla to watch the sundown. Get yourself a *mate* set and you'll fit right in. Teenagers and twenty-somethings will come back after dinner and stay there till the early hours.

The Eagle (El Aguila), Villa Argentina Half an hour walk from Atlantida, overlooking the beach from the top of a cliff sits the Eagle. A handmade building in the form of a stone eagle-head, this folly was built in 1945 by our Italian casino owner. The story goes that he used to hang out there with family and friends, but the symbolism and the year of construction have led to rumours of Nazi spies, temples and cosmic energy centres. None have ever been proved. If the Eagle is open you can visit inside. If it's closed, no worries. It's the whimsy, and the speculation that you can indulge in as you walk back to your hotel, that's the most fun.

Cristo Obrero Church, Estación Atlantida Architecture appreciators from all over the world travel to Atlantida to visit the Cristo Obrero Church which lies to the north of the IB highway. The church was built by Eladio Dieste (1917-2000). The world-renowned Uruguayan engineer and architect designed every-day structures in brick—grain silos, factory sheds, schools[8] and churches—considered exceptionally elegant feats of engineering even today. With its curved brick exterior, the interior of the church is even more stunning especially in the afternoon sunlight. R 11 km 164. 5 minutes by car. Open Saturdays 2-4.30pm

---

8   Recognise Dieste's work while you are in Uruguay www.guruguay.com/dieste-rural-schools

Arroyo Solis Chico, Parque del Plata The ever-changing mouth of the Solis Chico river (*arroyo* means river) could be something out of a film set for Lawrence of Arabia. The reflections on the water are mesmerising. Walk up river to the abandoned iron railway bridge which used to carry passengers to Punta del Este. At the Solis Chico Boating Club you'll see the statue of a large cartoon frog. No, the alt-right has not reached Uruguay. This is a monument to El Sapo Ruperto, a fictional detective and favourite of Uruguayan children's literature. On Sunday nights between the highway and river, Parque del Plata's *candombe* drummers rehearse. Usually drumming groups are out around sundown. Just follow your ears. The river is a three-mile (5 km) walk along the beach from Atlantida.

Wine-tasting at Viñedo de los Vientos See *Wine Country, East coast* Just beyond Cristo Obrero church

Private wine tours See *Wine Country, Private wine tours*

What you should know

There's not much to do The Costa de Oro appeals to people looking for a very self-contained holiday. There's not a huge amount to do other than strolling down to the water front and along the waterline. Its proximity to Montevideo makes it a great spot for people looking to kick-back and relax with occasional forays into the capital for music and culture. Though who are you kidding right? You're just going to zonk out in a hammock to the sound of the birds and the sea.

The rest of the beaches of Costa del Oro The beachtowns east of La Floresta all have very small populations and minimal tourism infrastructure. I haven't been able to find hotels or restaurants that stay open all year round that meet my standards. It pains me to leave out almost 25 miles (40 km) of coastline but until I can report differently, so be it. By all means rent houses in those areas—you will find great deals off season—but expect to be self-reliant as you will find little in the way of supermarkets, and few or no restaurants and bars.

To rent a car or not? If you want to do day trips and get around then you definitely need a car. There are buses that link the beach towns but they are infrequent. To day trip to Montevideo or Punta del Este you usually have to wait for your bus on the side of the highway. If you prefer not to drive, stay at a hotel with half or full board (the two I have selected are perfect for that) or rent a house in one of the larger beach towns. However do not let me prejudice you against smaller beach settlements. Quiz your prospective rental owner on the proximity and quality of local facilities.

Nightlife A few of the larger towns like La Floresta and Atlantida have some nightlife in January, less so by February. In the off season there is very little nightlife, other than occasional initiatives by folks like Salvador Bar.

Algae and jelly fish During the hottest months there may be occasional cases of algae in river water. Lifeguards will put out red flags with a green cross on them and you should avoid bathing. In February there may be an occasional jelly fish (they are very small, just a few inches across) invasion.

When to visit

The Costa de Oro is a great destination all year round which is why so many Europeans and North Americans are starting to settle here. As mentioned the facilities in many beach towns are basic and decent restaurants limited. Off season is a great time to visit Costa de Oro for the tranquillity and rental discounts.

Where to stay

Though the Costa del Oro was in the tourism vanguard a century ago, it has lacked for good hotel options for the last few decades but happily just in the last couple of years things have changed.

Santoral Posada, Atlantida

Santoral is a six-room boutique hotel in a 1920s listed house on the rambla. The owners are part of the hip set from Montevideo connected to the arts and music scene. Décor is quirky vintage with touches from past travels to Angola and Portugal. Though the house has been carefully preserved, the bathrooms have been radically redone with high-pressure showers. Beds are large with luxurious pillows. Breakfast includes a selection of fresh fruit including pineapple and strawberries out of season and high value items such as almonds. "American breakfast" is available on request. There's a (very) small swimming pool next to the restaurant for exclusive use by guests. The hotel has a Portuguese-Mediterranean cuisine restaurant on site. The location is incredibly central. Holiday makers looking for a contemporary hotel in a traditional resort favoured by the locals will appreciate this eclectic locale. Several of the staff speak excellent English. Note that from Mar 1-Dec 19 they only open weekends. Write to Laura at contacto@santoral.com.uy or visit www.santoral.com.uy

Hotel Fortín de Santa Rosa, Santa Rosa

The iconic hotel originally run by the current owner's grandfather is styled like a fort with a portcullis entrance and a mini turret where the King and Queen suites are located. Overlooking the beach, rooms have views of the sea or the surrounding pineforest. Inside the Andalucian patio brims with flowering vines. The lounge-bar has antique furniture with hip animal print upholstery, chessboard tiling and a huge fireplace. Breakfast has fresh fruit, good strong coffee and French preserves. Gloria makes freshly-baked goods like traditional *pasta frola* or scones each morning. Bacon and eggs on request. Santa Rosa is secluded. If you don't come with your own transport, it makes sense to arrange half or full board. The Fortín is perfect for starting or ending your trip. The airport is under ten miles away and they offer transfers. Two new cabins with decks overlooking the beach are ideal for 1-2 people. Owner Jose did some highschool in Michigan. His English is rusty but enthusiastic. Write to Jose at hola@fortindesantarosa.com.uy or visit www.fortindesantarosa.com.uy

Where to eat

Salvador Bar, Cuchilla Alta

This rustic bar two blocks from the beach is run by young people looking to "do stuff with love and decentralise from Montevideo". The restaurant opened seven years ago (an eternity by Uruguayan beach standards) and focuses on serving quality food with local, seasonal ingredients. They organise eclectic live music and art shows once a month during winter when things get tough economically on the coast to bring in more public. The whole town—grannies, hippies, hipsters, little kids—attends. IB km 72. Check their Facebook page to see if you'll get lucky enough to experience a live event or ask Laura at laura.benvenuto@live.com

Don Vito, Atlantida

One of my favourite restaurants in Costa de Oro. It's a traditional *parrilla* (grill) and so popular it opens every day of the week all year round. It's become more pricey but the quality of the food, particularly the meat and the desserts is outstanding and portions enormous. I particularly love the grilled lamb (*cordero*), the *bife ancho* (a melt-in-your-mouth steak usually reserved for export) and the pork ribs (*pechito de cerdo*). The waiters are so friendly (and cultured—ours loosely quoted Kant to an indecisive member of our party). Desserts come from Baipa, a bakery in town, also highly recommended. info@donvito.com.uy

Santoral Restaurant, Atlantida

Before opening Santoral, chefs Yamandú Gallo and Laura Charlone ran a well-known restaurant in what was to become trendy Parque Rodó in Montevideo. Always slightly ahead of the curve, Santoral is the first gourmet restaurant of its kind on the Costa de Oro. They serve lunch, dinner and Uruguay-style high tea. Having lived in Angola and Lisbon, their cuisine is Portuguese-influenced including braised meats and salt cod (*bacalao*). Pastas are home-made. Afternoon tea is pastry chef Laura's baby and includes that Uruguayan favourite—the toasted cheese sandwich—as well as a selection of sweets. Seating is indoor and outdoor around a hypnotic brazier. The owners are friends with a lot of musicians so there's always an interesting choice of background music. Open daily for high tea and dinner, Sat and Sun lunch, closed Mondays; off season (Mar1-Dec 19) Thur-Sun high tea, Sat and Sun lunch, Fri and Sat dinner. Write to Laura at contacto@santoral.com.uy or visit www.santoral.com.uy

Restaurante Fortín de Santa Rosa, Santa Rosa

It's worth checking out this restaurant for the location alone—a replica Andalucian fort in a small forest—though the food is pretty good too. Serving "healthy food made in the moment", fish is caught locally, there's no deep frying and only olive oil is used. Saturday nights may include live music—which could feature Jose, the owner, who was a well-known mover and shaker of "the Uruguayan night" till he chose the quieter pace of the Fortin. Open (Nov-April) daily for lunch and dinner; off season Sat and Sun lunch and Sat dinner. Open for hotel guests 365 days of the year. Reserve at hola@fortindesantarosa.com.uy

During summer, the Fortín opens up an outdoor beachstand with a fantastic view of the sea and Atlantida in the distance serving typical Uruguayan beach food—*chivitos*, *milanesas*, fries and ice-cold beer. Open daily Dec 15-Mar 15

Also see Where to eat in *Beaches, El Pinar* These great eateries are ten minutes drive

How to get to Costa de Oro

Fortín de Santa Rosa **IB km 41.500** Atlantida **IB km 45.500**

Driving It is very simple to get to any of the beaches on the Costa de Oro as they all lie directly south of the IB highway. You just need to know the km marker number. Beach names are clearly signposted. The first Neptunia is at the 34 km marker and the last Jaureguiberry at the 79 km marker.

Coming from the airport The Carrasco International Airport is virtually at the start of the IB itself at what would be the 20 km marker. So if you are going to Fortín de Santa Rosa (km 41.5) you know you have just over 21 km to drive to your destination. So simple and so quick!

Coming by bus Numerous buses leave every day from Montevideo Tres Cruces bus station and the airport to the Costa de Oro. You will be dropped off on the IB highway at your km marker.

El Pinar, Canelones

Close to the international airport lies an unbroken ten-mile beach fringed with residential suburbs of chalets and neat green lawns. The beach is broad with that ultra-fine powdery white sand typical of Uruguay's river beaches. The neighbourhoods make up the second most populous area of Uruguay after Montevideo in what was designated a city in the 1990s and is known as Ciudad de la Costa (Coastal City). This area of former holiday homes became a satellite for the capital in the 80s and 90s. The settlements have grown and fused together so that only a local really knows where one neighbourhood ends and the next begins. The nicest settlement is El Pinar (km 30), carefully planned in the late 40s so plots are larger than average and even humbler houses are surrounded by lovely green lawns and pine-tree forest. As one inhabitant told to me, it's half-nature, half-civilization.

What you should know

You're on holiday in El Pinar??? Prepare yourself for absolutely noone to believe that you came from abroad to stay here. Uruguayans conceive of Ciudad de la Costa as a satellite city, end of story. Crazy considering the lovely beach and solitude so close to the capital. You are pioneers!

Services have not kept apace with the population explosion. Most of the roads off the main road are dirt with serial potholes and they may flood during intense rains.

Also refer to *Beaches, Atlantida & Costa de Oro* The issues raised in the *What you should know* section apply here.

Things to do

The main reason to stay in El Pinar currently is the proximity to the airport. If you decide to stay for any length of time you'll definitely want to check out Montevideo 30-40 minutes away and surrounding beachtowns.

Where to stay

The first business people that set up a hotel on the beach in Ciudad de la Costa could be in for a nice surprise. But at the time of writing, the only enterprising souls are the folks at El Bambú.

Posada El Bambú

This cosy four-room B&B is a five-minute drive from the airport in a quiet residential neighbourhood just ten minutes walk through pinetrees to the dunes and beach and two first-rate restaurants. A tiny splash pool is the central feature of the wooden outdoor deck. All rooms have air-conditioning and some have pool or garden views. The owners Omar and Adriana spent their childhood holidays in El Pinar and moved here over two decades ago. They are incredibly warm and friendly and Adriana who is well-travelled herself speaks great English. El Bambú is a great location for people who want some peace and quiet, stay with a local family and still be close enough to Montevideo to be able to make day trips in under an hour or as a last port before taking the plane back home. They offer free airport transfers and bikes, essential for getting around the neighbourhood. Omar grows his own marijuana plants and guests are welcome to sample. Write to Adriana at posadaelbambu@gmail.com or visit www.posadaelbambu.com

Where to eat

Well-heeled residents of Montevideo are moving from upper-class neighbourhood Carrasco to El Pinar for additional peace and quiet and lower land prices. These two great eateries make a perfect pit-stop on your way east.

Arazá Restó, El Pinar

Arazá is a native fruit of Uruguay and almost an emblem of the slow food movement here. Chef Diego Cáceres has taken slow food as his way of life. Wanting more time with his son, he left a successful parrilla in Montevideo to set up this small gourmet bistro. He lives upstairs and his resto is not a business, it's his way of life. The menu is limited with a focus on seafood, risottos and fresh fish. In season desserts may include native fruits. Fresh bread baked on the premises is served daily. The wooden house has a lovely garden for outside dining. Children are especially welcome and Diego happy to modify his menu for the small ones. He was the bassist for one of Uruguay's most innovative percussionists, Nico Arnicho[9] and top musicians are regularly invited to play acoustic sets. Open daily for dinner, Sat and Sun lunch, closed Mondays. Reserve at diecamo@gmail.com

Parador Burdeos, El Pinar

Roman used to rent jet skis on this almost-tropical sandbank on the Pando river. A carpenter by trade he built a beachshack (or *parador*) and started selling seafood snacks to his hungry costumers. The construction got bigger. "He likes big stuff" his right hand person told me and an enormous iron buoy turned into a massive fireplace is the dramatic centrepiece of what is nowadays a luxury restaurant. During high season reservations are essential. Roman who still pads around barefoot says he prefers off season when he can hang out with clients. Just 30 minutes from Montevideo it's a piece of tropical paradise. If money's no object, visit twice—day time and night time are completely different, magical experiences. Open daily (Nov-Easter) noon till midnight; off season Thu-Sat noon till midnight, Sunday noon till 8pm. Lunch

---

9   *The Guru'Guay Guide to Montevideo* recommends more than forty live acts that you can get to catch when you are in town. Nico Arnicho is one of those featured. You have to check him out when you visit.

ends 4pm, dinner starts 8pm. Reserve at restaurantburdeos@gmail.com

How to get to El Pinar

Av Giannattasio km 30 Airport (10m) Montevideo (40-50 m)

Driving From Montevideo follow the rambla out of the city and hug the coast. The rambla becomes the Rambla Costanera of Ciudad de la Costa. At the very end of the rambla lies El Pinar. From the east El Pinar is the first turning left after the tollbooth over the Arroyo Pando.

From the airport Maybe I am also falling to the prejudice of native Montevideans but if you have just arrived in Uruguay, I'd recommend heading further east to the beach rather than staying in El Pinar. However it makes a great end to your holiday as you'll be just a 5-10 minute drive to the airport. Carrasco International Airport is just off R101 where it intersects with the IB.

Bus Take any bus to 'El Pinar' (CUTCSA and COPSA) which travels along Paysandú street, Av Italia or Rivera in Montevideo. Most go along Av Giannattasio. The bus terminal is on the Arroyo Pando itself. There are a couple of buses which take the more scenic Rambla Costanera. You can descend at any bus stop or *parada* (they are numbered). Parada 13 is in the centre of El Pinar.

Montevideo

Montevideo is a charming city, especially if you have spent time in hectic Buenos Aires. It's calmer, more laid back, and locals take advantage of the river all year round. You'll see kite surfers and families along the city's ten beaches, people heading to the bars and cafés to take in the sunset, and the massive fifteen-mile rambla is perfect for cycling, roller-blading, getting in a run or just walking off the awesome food and drink.

The beaches have great quality sand—it's remarkably fine and powdery and white. Despite this, don't think I am recommending you plan to come to Montevideo specifically for a beach holiday. There are far more glorious beaches further east. However as neighbourhoods like Parque Rodó, Pocitos, Malvín and Carrasco have their own beaches and any beach is accessible by bike, bus or walking in minutes, it would be crazy not to head down to the *playa*. Thousands of Uruguayans can't be wrong.

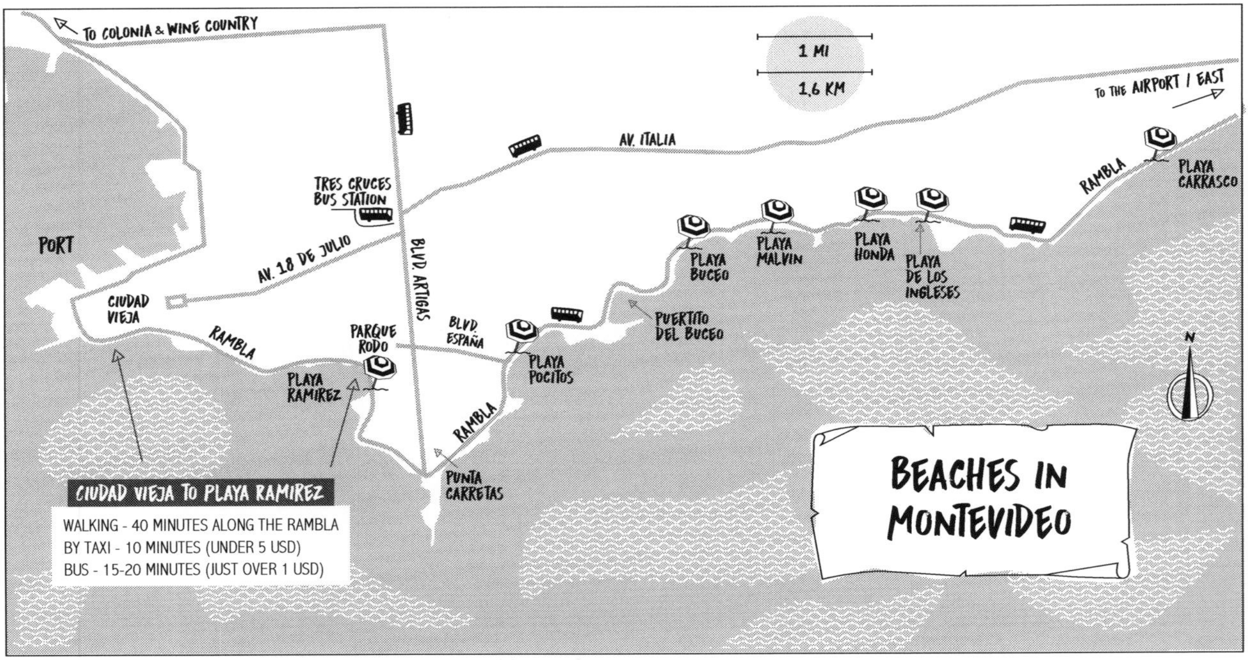
TO COLONIA & WINE COUNTRY
1 MI
1,6 KM
TO THE AIRPORT / EAST
AV. ITALIA
TRES CRUCES BUS STATION
PORT
AV. 18 DE JULIO
BLVD. ARTIGAS
CIUDAD VIEJA
RAMBLA
PARQUE RODO
BLVD. ESPAÑA
PLAYA POCITOS
PLAYA RAMIREZ
PUERTITO DEL BUCEO
PLAYA BUCEO
PLAYA MALVIN
PLAYA HONDA
PLAYA DE LOS INGLESES
PLAYA CARRASCO
RAMBLA
RAMBLA
PUNTA CARRETAS
N
CIUDAD VIEJA TO PLAYA RAMIREZ
WALKING - 40 MINUTES ALONG THE RAMBLA
BY TAXI - 10 MINUTES (UNDER 5 USD)
BUS - 15-20 MINUTES (JUST OVER 1 USD)
BEACHES IN MONTEVIDEO

The beaches

Playa Ramírez is a broad sandy beach right on the edge of Montevideo's oldest park, Parque Rodó (which has two fun fairs and the National Museum of Visual Arts, Uruguay's largest collection of art) so there's plenty to do if you get bored of the sand. The water is very shallow and ideal for children. This is the best beach from which to watch the sunset. **Playa Pocitos** is a long beach with lovely white sand popular with its middle-class residents. The water gets reasonably deep quickly so it makes for good swimming. Pocitos is bordered by apartment buildings (think Tel Aviv or Nice) which cast a long shadow over most of the sand the last few hours of the day which is a relief or an annoyance depending on the season. **Playa Buceo** is a flat beach typically used for sports. It's good to combine with a visit to the Buceo Cemetery

(Montevideo's undiscovered rival to Buenos Aires' famous Recoleta Cemetery). **Playa Malvín** is a wide very flat beach popular with kite-surfers. There's a rather good *parador* serving meals and drinks. **Playa Honda** in Punta Gorda is a smallish beach with deeper waters (*honda* means deep). Here a surfer might find waves. **Playa de los Ingleses** also in Punta Gorda can get very busy during summer and given that it is small, you feel the crowds more than you will elsewhere. The Punta Gorda and Carrasco sports club overlooks the beach and has a restaurant with a large terrace. The Fair Sailing Centre[10] attached to the club offers sailing and wind-surfing lessons and boat and board hire at ridiculously low prices. As residents of Montevideo's most exclusive neighbourhood typically have access to private pools, **Playa Carrasco** tends to be deserted most of the year.

Things to do

The Old City (Ciudad Vieja) (see-you-DAD vee-AY-zhah) is Montevideo's historic neighbourhood. It is packed with art galleries, antique shops, auction houses, enchanting book stores, quaint bars and historic cafes and surrounded on three sides by the waters of River Plate. The Old City is home to the capital's best eateries including the Port Market, dubbed Disneyland for carnivores by The Guardian.

Photographers paradise It's been called a city made for black and white. Feast on art-Deco, Belle Époque and modernist architecture. Plan lots of time for just walking around.

Andes 1972 Museum[11] The story of the young Uruguayans who survived 72 days in the Andes after their plane crashed is one of the great human survival stories of the twentieth century and a tale of Uruguayan values—teamwork, solidarity and friendship. The exhibit—in English, Spanish and German—is sensitively done and incredibly moving. If you only go to one museum make it this one. You may run into one of the survivors having a coffee—the director is friends with several of them. Open Mon-Fri 10am-5pm, Sat 10am-3pm. 200 pesos.

---

10   www.guruguay.com/boat-board-rental
11   www.guruguay.com/andes-1972-museum

Tristan Narvaja market This antique and flea market starts at the corners of Av 18 de Julio and Tristan Narvaja. The side streets are more interesting with vendors laying out their wares on blankets. Beware of pickpockets on Tristan Narvaja itself. Sundays 8am-2pm

Old City walking tours There's a free walking tour that goes every day from the Plaza Independencia at 11am and 2.30pm (look out for the red shirts). For a more personalised experience, our favourite tour guide is Christine Dulin[12]. With her you'll climb the iconic Palacio Salvo for birds eye views of the city. Get a feel for Montevideo's vibrant carnival and Afro-Uruguayan culture. Learn juicy historical background and secrets behind the city's most beautiful architecture. And most importantly taste that mate drink that everyone absolutely everyone is carrying around.

Carnival tours[13] Uruguay has the longest carnival in the world. It starts with a number of parades and continues with nightly shows called *tablados*. And the whole thing goes on for forty nights. Carnival in Uruguay is totally different to the Brazilian version. Ours is family-oriented, has virtually zero tourists, a touch of politics and a lot of humour. We recommend local culture-vulture Christine Dulin's tours to carnival rehearsals in January and then carnival proper in February and early March. Unmissable.

City bike tour[14] Orient yourself to the city with this private biking tour which includes the *rambla,* a photo shoot at the emblematic 'Montevideo' sign, Parque Rodó, the Centenario Stadium where the first World Cup was played, Montevideo's main street, the hundred-year old Agricultural Market and the National Assembly where the government legalised marijuana production—a world first.

Football tours and matches[15] Take a tour through Uruguay's footballing past including the Centenario stadium. It's a great way to spend the afternoon, and I say that as someone who doesn't like football.

---

12 www.guruguay.com/listings/private-walking-tour-old-city
13 www.gurguay.com/listings/carnival-tour
14 www.guruguay.com/listings/montevideo-bike-tour
15 www.guruguay.com/listings/uruguay-soccer-history-tour

Wine-tasting in Montevideo and Canelones See *Wine Country, Montevideo & Canelones*

Private wine tours See *Wine Country, Private wine tours*

What you should know

Stay at least three nights to really get a flavour of the city. Even better, stay a week or ten days, head out to those wineries—and sleep some siestas. The city needs to be slowly savoured to feel its essence.

Montevideans take their public holidays seriously Whereas beach towns in the rest of Uruguay are at their busiest over the end of year holidays, Montevideo is extremely quiet. Between Christmas and the New Year, many bars and restaurants are closed. January, especially the first two weeks, is also very quiet. Enjoy the peace and go to the beach, walk or cycle the *rambla* and make day trips. Then Carnival starts in the last week of January and Montevideo's intense cultural activity is back on.

When to visit

Live music Montevideo has many world-class live music events any night of the week especially between March and up to the Christmas holidays. There is most choice Thursday to Saturday. Contact the Guru on Facebook[16] for recommendations while you are here.

Museums and galleries Many museums open Monday to Friday. Art museums and galleries open weekends, usually Tuesday to Sunday.

The Old City is best experienced on weekdays when it is at its most bustling.

The most interesting market Tristan Narvaja is on Sunday mornings.

Carnival The official carnival season lasts a minimum 40 nights from the last week of January, throughout February to approximately the first week in March. You can see *candombe* drumming and dancing groups practising on the street most nights of the

---

16   www.facebook.com/guruguay1

week all year around and carnival groups (such as the popular *murgas*) perform in theatres or other events throughout the year.

Where to stay

Hotel Alma Historica

Alma Historica—which means 'historic soul'—is a luxury fifteen-room boutique hotel set on Plaza Zabala, Montevideo's most romantic park. The 1920s art-Deco townhouse was lovingly renovated by its Italian owners opening in 2014. It went straight onto Condé Nast's hot list. The New York Times praised it as "an antiques-filled haven that bridges historic charm and modern efficiency". Each room is uniquely decorated, inspired by Uruguayan artists and creators including an aviator, an actress and a tango singer. Rooms have views of the plaza, the River Plate, the port and the Old City. A roof terrace has a jacuzzi and massage room, and there's an elegant but inviting lounge for relaxing and meetings. www.almahistoricahotel.com using GURU $$$$

Casa Sarandi

Run by the author of the Guru'Guay guidebooks, you won't be better oriented to the city than if you stay in our award-winning art-Deco guesthouse in the heart of Montevideo's Old City. Guestrooms have private bathrooms, queen-size beds and balconies with views of the Old City and the River Plate. You'll have access to a fully-equipped kitchen and shared living room. Perfect for the independent traveller. On arrival the Guru or a family member will be there to greet you. Every day I will personally send you recommendations of things to do based on your preferences. Thousands of people visit Guru'Guay each month but when you stay with us you get the inside scoop personally—even before you arrive if that's what you need. Always breaking-ground in tourism Casa Sarandi was the first accommodation in Uruguay to become part of the Bud & Breakfast network. Write to Karen at info@casasarandi.com or visit www.casasarandi.com $$$

Nomade Suites

Roberto lived a nomadic life in high finance and Wall Street for twenty years until he decided to return to his native Uruguay and set up six eclectically-furnished rental units in a 1920s three-storey French-style building on Sarandi, the main pedestrian street through Montevideo's Old City. Each suite has a separate bedroom, kitchenette and private bathroom. The four superior suites over Sarandi have picture windows onto the pedestrian street below. Guests have access to a roof top deck with sun beds, a typical Uruguayan barbecue and views right across the Old City and of the River Plate. A group of three couples or a family can comfortably rent three units and take the entire floor. Write to Roberto at hello@nomadesuites.com or visit www.nomadesuites.com $$$

Where to eat

Sin Pretensiones, Ciudad Vieja

Traditional Uruguayan comfort food at great prices cooked exquisitely and served in a vintage furniture store. Twenty-something chef Guillermina grew up in the hospitality business—her family ran restaurants in Punta and a top Argentine ski resort—and it shows. She takes typical Uruguayan dishes and bumps them up to a gourmet level. Her crunchy skinny pizzas are topped with smoked salmon or *jamón crudo* (Serrano ham) and the freshest arugula. Her *postres*—desserts—are to die for and there's even vegan ice cream. If you want something that's not on the menu—like a gourmet *chivito* or *mate* (this traditional Uruguayan drink is not usually served in a restaurant), or if you have dietary restrictions just advise the multilingual wait staff. Sarandi 366. Open Mon-Fri 9.30am-6pm. Write to Mariana at info@sinpretensiones.com.uy

Es Mercat, Ciudad Vieja

I'll wager that this is the best fish restaurant in the entire city. The *merluza negra* (sea bass) solely seasoned with rock salt is particularly amazing. To have the best culinary experience ask chef Roberto Connio to select what you'll eat. For two, he'll generally recommend a couple of appetizers and one main course as main dishes are large enough to share. A chef from Texas told me that he was so blown away that by the time his main course arrived, "my eyes just filled up". Bring an appetite and cash, as no credit cards are accepted. Colón and Piedras. Open daily lunch, Thur-Sat dinner (extra evenings in summer). Write to Facundo at esmercatrestobar@hotmail.com

Alquimista, Carrasco

Alquimista is an elegant "gastropub with rooms" which just happens to be in Montevideo. The turreted former 1920s holiday home opened in 2017, and the restaurant and tearoom became an instant must-visit in chi-chi Carrasco, Montevideo's most expensive barrio just ten minutes from the airport. The British-Uruguayan owners are seriously invested in local cuisine and wine. No imported products and absolutely no Argentine wine are permitted. They use only the very best local ingredients and their thousand-bottle wine cellar only features top quality independent producers featured in this guide like Viñedo de los Vientos and El Legado (though this being Uruguay bottles start at 15 USD). The six guestrooms are exquisitely decorated with antique furniture and rates a quarter of what you'd pay in other parts of the world. Just one block from Carrasco's long sandy beach, this little inn is a floral oasis in the city and a great stop-off before you catch your plane home. Bolivia 1323. Open Wed-Sun lunch (12.30-4.30pm), Wed-Sat tea (4.30-8pm) Reservations essential. Write to Carolina at info@alquimistamontevideo.com

How to get to Montevideo

See *Getting to Uruguay, From Buenos Aires*

Colonia del Sacramento & Carmelo

Colonia del Sacramento is a colonial town with UNESCO heritage status and Carmelo is an important wine-producing town in the department of Colonia (see *Wine Country, Carmelo*). Both towns have much more to offer than their very pleasant river beaches. However it gives the Guru opportunity to cover Colonia del Sacramento, an essential entry in any Uruguayan guidebook.

The beaches

The most well-known beach in **Carmelo** is **Playa Seré** in the town centre. It's not particularly lovely but the trees offer pleasant shade on a hot day. If you are staying in Colonia Estrella **Zagarzazú** (say za-gar-za-ZOO) is a very quiet beach ideal for paddling and walking with a forested backdrop.

The sand is super fine and powdery white. The water is indisputably river water, brown due to the silt it is carrying in suspension, typical of the very mature rivers in this part of the world. I'll confess the first time I came across a beach of this sort I was reluctant to venture into the water. However once you see everyone else diving in during the summer there's really not much to hold you back.

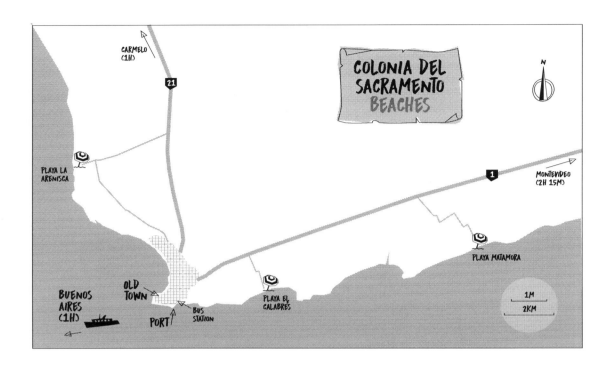

Colonia del Sacramento has a number of beaches in the old town and also stretching out north of the town centre. Perfect for taking long walks or a post-lunch siesta. If you have transport, friends of mine who've lived in Colonia for twenty years particularly recommend two beaches off the Ruta 1. **Playa Matamora** (R1 km 164.5, turn off 'Riachuelo') east of Colonia is particularly quiet and unspoiled, only reachable on a dirt track which passes by Antik, a small antiques shop which serves afternoon tea. The owners speak English and have great tips on local artesans to visit. It's a lovely place to spend the afternoon. If you don't fancy the river water **Playa El Calabrés** (R1 km 173.5) is a broad beach with dunes and a huge freshwater quarry pool marvellous for swimming. The dilapidated concrete quay where fishermen spend their days is also impressive. **La Arenisca** is north of Colonia on the road to Carmelo (R21 km 184, turn at the sign 'El Caño Piedra de los Indios' and drive till you hit the river). The beach is picturesque, with a little island out front and good for fishing.

Things to do

Carmelo See *Wine Country, Carmelo*

Colonia del Sacramento

Colonia del Sacramento was founded by the Portuguese in 1680. The historic quarter (*casco histórico*) is full of old stone houses, cobbled streets and antique cars and is a delightful destination any time of year. The town was awarded UNESCO World Heritage status in 1995.

Climb to the top of the 1857 lighthouse to enjoy the view Built on the ruins of an old convent, the lower half of the lighthouse is strangely square and the upper part is the cylindrical shape as you'd expect.

The emblematic Calle de los Suspiros There are different theories regarding the origin of the name of the Street of Sighs—that it was the final path of prisoners condemned to death and taken to the river to be shot, or that it was named for the sound of the wind blowing off the river, or that this was where the brothels of Colonia were located in the 1900s.

The seven tiny museums in the Old Town may be more interesting for the old buildings they inhabit rather than their limited exhibits. You can buy a ticket which allows you to enter them all for fifty pesos from the Museo Municipal at the western end of the Plaza Mayor. Open daily 11.15am-4.15pm closed Tuesdays

Private wine tour to Carmelo See *Wine Country, Private wine tours*

But Colonia more than anything is a place to contemplate. One of the best vantage points being the harbour jetty which dates from 1866.

What you should know

Colonia or Colonia del Sacramento? The town is officially called Colonia del Sacramento though it is often referred to as Colonia for short. Just to confuse things Colonia is the name of the department where Colonia del Sacramento is located.

How much time do you need to explore Colonia del Sacramento? The town is small and compact so you can easily explore it in 4-5 hours including lunch, though it is a lovely place to spend a few nights.

Hiring a car If you are planning to stay in the centre of Colonia del Sacramento and then go direct to Montevideo, you don't need a car. Buses are cheap (apx. 12 USD one way) and have Wi-Fi. Kick back and let someone else do the driving.

Baggage drop The bus station right next to the port has a luggage deposit. You can leave your bags there for just a few dollars while you explore the town. The port does not have luggage facilities.

You cannot buy a through ticket Buenos Aires-Montevideo and do a stop-off in Colonia Yes, the ticket says 'via Colonia' but stopping off is just not allowed. Transportation company bureaucracy. Sigh. However there is a simple solution. Buy a ferry ticket to Colonia. When you arrive, head over to the bus station next door (and leave your bags at left luggage) and buy a bus ticket to Montevideo for later in the day.

When to visit

Colonia is a popular day-trip for visitors from Buenos Aires so avoid going on weekends if you want to experience the tiny city at its best.

Where to stay

Colonia Suite

Colonia Suite is an oasis of peace and calm in a beautifully-renovated old building on a quiet tree-lined avenue five minutes from the port and the old town. Guestrooms are enormous, full of light and breezy with painted floor boards, soft rush matting and rugs and an eclectic mix of art. The multilingual owner Fred is an artist himself. The large bathrooms have lashings of hot water and huge soft white towels. Each room has a kitchenette with small fridge and tea and *mate* are provided. There's a lovely selection of books and games in the lounge. It's perfect to sit and relax to the sound of the leaves in the trees and the occasional squawk of a wild parrot. Breakfast is much better than the standard Uruguayan B&B breakfast with fresh juice, fruit, cold cuts, eggs and home-made jams served in the garden. Write to Fred at coloniasuite@gmail.com or visit www.coloniasuite.com $$$

La Posadita de La Plaza

Brazilian Eduardo moved to Colonia and set up a photography store right on the main plaza in the old town. A collage artist as well as photographer he quickly started filling the back passages of the store and then decided to build upstairs. Suddenly a warren of rooms filled with pop-art and 60s memorabilia exploded in a totally unexpected space in a colonial town. There's a clock on the shop front that has an hour-hand only. That is how time works in Uruguay, says Eduardo. His suggestions of where to eat and what to do in Colonia are always spot on. The Posadita has four guest rooms and a plunge pool. Not for traditionalists. Write to Eduardo at laposaditadelaplaza@gmail.com or visit www.posaditadelaplaza.com $$$$

Where to eat

Charco Bistró

At Charco you'll have a beautiful view of the water whether you sit inside or on the heated out-door terrace. It's an exclusive restaurant, the wait-staff are attentive and the food has certain pretensions. There's an extensive wine selection including Bouza and Garzón wines. Prices are steep but you should have a magical time. San Pedro 116. Open daily 8am-11pm closed between 4-7pm. Reservations info@charcohotel.com

Don Joaquin

Perhaps the best pizza I have ever tasted in Uruguay. The chefs cook in the window of this small restaurant where the locals go to eat. Prices are much more reasonable than almost anywhere in Colonia. What a shame it only opens in the evenings. 18 de julio 267. Open daily 8-12pm closed Mondays

El Buen Suspiro

A romantic little wine bar serving good quality local cheeses and cold cuts with wonderfully friendly service in Colonia's most emblematic cobbled street—the Street of Sighs. Calle de los Suspiros 90. Open daily 11.30am till midnight. Reservations suspiros90@gmail.com

MissFusión

A gastropub specialising in tapas and innovative cocktails using local and seasonal products. They also serve craft beers and regional wines. Chef and owner, Erika Valencillos who hails from Venezuela, speaks great English and French. She also offers cookery classes. Manuel Lobo 449. Open Tue-Sat evenings, Fri-Sat lunch closed Sundays and Mondays. Reservations barmissfusion@gmail.com

How to get to Colonia de Sacramento

R1 km 177 Montevideo (2 h 15 m) Carmelo (1 h) Flores (2 h 30 m) Florida (3 h)

Driving From Montevideo take the rambla out of Montevideo, take Ruta 1 and just drive straight for 177 km. From Carmelo, take R21. From estancias in Flores and Florida, take the advice of your hosts.

Bus From Montevideo buses (COT and TURIL) leave at least every hour (2 h 45 m). From Carmelo buses (Berrutti) leave every 1-2 hours (1 h 30 m) with less frequency on weekends.

Ferry Several ferries (Buquebus, Seacat and Colonia Express) travel daily between Buenos Aires and Colonia del Sacramento (50 m). Ferry prices may spiral on public holidays and weekends. The bus station is right next to the port.

For Carmelo See *Wine Country, Carmelo, How to get to Carmelo*

Ranches

Ninety-five percent of the interior of Uruguay is devoted to agriculture and criss-crossed by railroads built with British capital and knowhow in the later half of the 1800s and abandoned in the 1980s. Roads are deserted. The few souls you pass on the road include gauchos who will wave to you. It's possible to daytrip into deep Uruguay but I'd encourage you to consider taking a few days to slow right down. In consultation with folks born and bred in the countryside I travelled extensively and selected six very different estancias—as ranches are called in Uruguay—and an inn specialising in horseriding especially for you lovely readers.

How long to stay

Plan to spend three or four nights, enjoy the serenity of the countryside, ride a few trails and allow the peace to seep into your soul. Horse enthusiasts will want to stick around for longer. At a working ranch a three-night stay will give you the opportunity of a full half-day riding on the sierra, a day experiencing working on the estancia with the animals and a day to relax.

When to visit

Mid December-February Summer temperatures can average the high 90s (36°C) and reach the 100s (40-42°C). From mid morning till four in the afternoon it's too hot to do much other than read a book under a tree or head to the waterhole.

March-May Autumn is serene. There tends to be little wind on the sierras and you can be out till late with temperatures hovering in the mid 70s (23-24°C) during the day and pleasantly cool at night. Excellent time for birdwatching.

July *La Yerra* is one of the most important community and festive events in the country calendar. It is when cattle are branded and young bulls castrated. Ouch. Now you know you really are in gaucho territory.

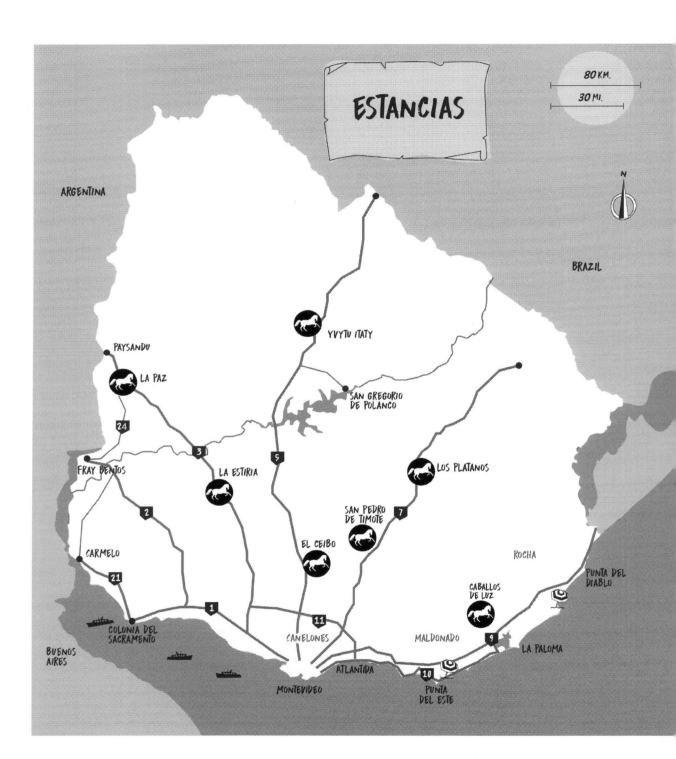

Late September to early December It's spring and the countryside explodes into bloom—everywhere you look the ground is yellow, white, pink and purple. Chicks are hatching. You can witness the birth of lambs and calves. Sheep shearing takes place in September and October. It's T-shirt weather during the day and cool at night. And it's not so hot for the horses so you can ride any time of day.

Also see *Practical Tips, Holidays & festivals*. The Guru has added a selection of recommended gaucho and folklore—country music and dance—festivals close to the estancias included in this guide, but there are hundreds of gaucho festivals throughout the year. Contact your estancia owner to find out what's on.

What you need to know

How much does an estancia stay cost? An estancia stay usually includes your room, four meals and all activities including a daily ride (optional). The rates in the estancias we recommend range between 100-135 USD per day (double room occupancy).[17]

GURU'GUAY

Get money off your estancia stay

10% off paying cash and 5% off with credit card when you mention Guru'Guay at time of booking

Cuisine Most estancias try to be self-sufficient and almost everything you eat they will have raised or grown in the purest air and soil conditions in the world. This is your chance to experience how Uruguayans in the countryside really eat (see *Practical Tips, Food & drink)*. Food is hearty and simple. There's a lot of meat—grilled, roasted and in stews. If it rains, it's inevitably time for *tortas fritas*, a donut-style snack. As vegetables are seasonal, canned fruit and vegetables may be part of a meal. Inevitably you will run into *galleta de campaña*, a type of biscuit designed to last for a week or more. It's actually surprisingly tasty when toasted with hot butter.

Flexible mealtimes One benefit of staying at a smaller estancia where the family cooks for you, is that they can adjust mealtimes to what you're used to. In fact as

---

17   Except Estancia Yvytu Itaty.

country people they are very happy to host Europeans and North Americans who go to bed at a reasonable hour. So while Uruguayans might sit down for dinner at ten, you can be tucked up in bed already.

Why choose all inclusive? Though most estancias will offer you a bed and breakfast or half board option, having visited all the establishments I would recommend full board. Restaurants in the interior are few and far between. Only Estancia La Paz is a thirty-minute drive to a restaurant worth leaving the ranch for.

What happens if the weather is bad? You'd be very unlucky. But most estancias will discount your bill if poor weather limits outdoor activities. Do check.

Unreliable internet Anywhere in the countryside, internet connectivity can be spotty. Don't go to the countryside with an online deadline.

Insects The countryside is full of insects. They are not dangerous but they can be bothersome particularly in summer when outdoor eating can become a challenge as you bat the flies away from your food. Only Los Platanos which is relatively high up has virtually no insects. In the sierras, Caballos de Luz has very few mosquitoes even in summer. If you want to avoid our six-legged friends visit May through November.

Sight-seeing To really get the feel of rural Uruguay it's important to take time to experience it—and take lots of siestas. After talking to multiple estancia owners, the reality is that most people arrive at the estancia and never leave during their entire stay. The Guru has included just one or two recommendations of places to visit on the way to your estancia or in the vicinity.

Do you need a car? You are likely to park your car on arrival and not move it again until you leave so it depends on your budget and preference. La Estiria and Los Platanos are just off the highway so you can get there easily by bus from Montevideo and they will pick you up on the road. The rest of the estancias are between 30-60 minutes drive from a highway on dirt roads. Most estancias offer reasonably priced transfers (certainly cheaper than a taxi) from the nearest town and Montevideo airport. As they are familiar with highways in poor condition, their transfers will be much quicker than you can drive yourself. Consult with the estancia for travel recommendations and transfers as they have the most up-to-date information.

Estancia El Ceibo, Florida

El Ceibo is a typical, South American sheep and cattle ranch set on the gently rolling plains of southern Uruguay. No roads pass by, apart from the miles-long private road to the ranch house. Other than the whinnying of the estancia's thoroughbred horses and a multitude of birds, the silence is absolute. And at night light pollution is minimal. Oh, the Milky Way!

The estancia building dates back to 1849 and thankfully has changed little. Even the wisteria which was planted back then still perfumes the central patio. El Ceibo has just five guestrooms, some with open fireplaces. The ranch is run by its owners, Carmen and Joselo, a couple originally from Florida, a nearby town. They moved to El Ceibo with their two sons over twenty years ago and run it as a working ranch as well as receiving visitors. Carmen speaks great English and is well-travelled. She can tell you a lot about Uruguay and the surrounding countryside. And she has a wicked, sophisticated sense of humour.

Most estancias take several hours to reach. El Ceibo is notable because it's little more than an hour from the international airport.

What you should know

El Ceibo relies on day tourism to generate income and may receive a day group during your stay. But not to worry. Estancia guests have exclusive use of the main estancia house. Groups are limited to an area behind the house out of view.

Those critters There are lots of insects at night all year round but rooms have screens on every window and romantic mosquito nets. I slept super soundly.

Things to do

Horseriding Joselo will take you out horseriding for an hour in the morning and in the afternoon every day. There's a wide track which goes for miles and the highest ground is about three miles from the estancia. As there are no mountains in Uruguay, just gentle hills, any elevation affords impressive views of the surrounding countryside.

Hiking There are few trails in Uruguay and abundant woodland is uncommon. However El Ceibo has varied terrain including over 120 acres of native woods. Take a two-hour trek following trails cut by Joselo on his 1950s Ford tractor.

Swimming Ten minutes walk across the property from the ranch is a lagoon—perfect for paddling in the four-person canoe—and a river which forms a natural rock pool which is safe for swimming and a sandy beach.

Birdwatching Where there's water and trees you'll see a lot of birds and El Ceibo is host to around one hundred species. Dawn is spectacular. The ranch has bird books and binoculars.

Fishing The most commonly caught species is the *tararira*—blue wolf fish.

What's nearby

Florida, capital of the department Florida is the provincial capital and the place where Uruguayan independence was first declared on August 25 1825, a day of big celebrations each year. Florida has one of the only cathedrals in Uruguay—home to the Virgin of the Thirty-Three, the patron saint of Uruguay. The Thirty-Three

Orientals were the liberators of Uruguay. Close to the Cathedral is the chapel of San Cono. San Cono is thought to bring good fortune and is a favourite with lottery enthusiasts. The chapel is filled with quirky testimonies of gratitude including offerings of bicycles, guitars and wedding dresses. The annual San Cono procession takes place every June 3 and is perhaps the most popular religious festival in infamously secular Uruguay[18]. Why not plan to visit during one of those festivals? You'll be virtually the only non-locals attending.

The murals of Vienticinco de Agosto The sleepiest little towns in Uruguay are full of surprises. 25 de agosto just 30 minutes from El Ceibo and an hour from Montevideo is home to almost a hundred murals by a French artist. The murals on shops and houses range from realist, to expressionist to the downright kitsch and have been painted on the request of their inhabitants. There's a DIY tour in English on Guru'Guay[19].

How to get to El Ceibo

R5 km 97.400 and off-road Montevideo (1 h) Flores (2 h) Colonia (3 h) Carmelo (4 h)

Driving From Montevideo take Ruta 5 to the town of Florida. Go past the Florida exit. At the roundabout turn right to El Ceibo. The drive along country lanes (16 km) takes 20 minutes and is very well sign-posted.

Bus Buses (Cita, Turismar and Bruno Hnos) from Montevideo to Florida are very frequent depending on the time of day (1-2 h). Arrange a transfer from the bus station with Carmen and Joselo for half the price of a taxi.

Airport Arrange your pickup with El Ceibo and you can be at the ranch within an hour of touch-down. Conversely Carmen has all the details of a leisurely three-hour bus (Las Marias) which winds through the countryside passing through little villages.

Contact Write to Carmen and Joselo at info@elceibo.com.uy or visit www.elceibo.com.uy

---

18 www.guruguay.com/why-uruguayans-celebrate-tourism-week-not-easter
19 www.guruguay.com/murals-25-de-agosto

San Pedro de Timote, Florida

For the last two centuries, San Pedro de Timote was a country estate owned by the country's most prominent agriculturalists and the pride of Uruguay. Today it's Uruguay's best-known estancia and a charming country hotel which retains the atmosphere of a stately country home.

More than two centuries of history

From their arrival in the 1600s the Jesuits worked huge swaths of South America including what is Uruguay today. Industrious as well as evangelising, they farmed and raised cattle so successfully, the Spanish king began to see them as competition and he expelled them from the continent in 1767. Ten years later, the crown sold almost half of the present day department of Florida to a Spaniard named Juan Francisco García de Zúñiga for the equivalent of just under thirty thousand dollars. It was a good deal. The agreement also included over 200,000 cows and their offspring and the right to graze even farther afield.

Unfortunately for García de Zúñiga, a decade later he fell foul of the king and lost his head. His descendants retained control of much of the land until the period of revolution prior to Uruguay's declaration of independence in 1825. Expecting the newly independent nation would confiscate Spanish-owned property, Juan's son did a deal with John Jackson, an English business man who had arrived in Uruguay almost twenty years earlier in what are known locally as the English Invasions[20]. Jackson snapped up over a quarter of a million acres from the García de Zuñigas and ran the land with an innovative and business-oriented mindset that would revolutionise agricultural management not just in Uruguay but in the world. But it was his great grandson, Alberto Gallinal Heber, who would found the estancia and make it a household name. Gallinal had a keen interest in genetics and was obsessed with improving livestock nationally. He used his round-the-world honeymoon tour to visit some of the foremost agricultural nations—USA, New Zealand, Australia and South Africa—returning home with premium livestock in the ship's hold. Running the national genetic registry and founding thorough-bred and livestock societies, he was significantly responsible for the impressive animals you see all over the country today. He was also the first to understand the importance of fertilizers and import them to Uruguay. Agricultural experts, engineers, politicians and European royalty flocked to San Pedro for much of the twentieth century, fascinated to find out what Gallinal was up to next.

Gallinal was very wealthy and not adverse to enjoying his money but he had a deep social conscience. He was responsible for two emblematic social welfare initiatives which remain hugely important today. MEVIR gave thousands of rural families the opportunity to form cooperatives and build their own houses and the Plan Gallinal-Dieste built over 220 rural schools[21], many of which are still in use.

Back at home, Gallinal was a stern, patriarchal leader. All the children on the estancia —both the workers' and Gallinal's own children—went to school on the estancia. He personally oversaw their homework. Beto the gaucho has lived his entire life at San Pedro. He was born in what is now Room 13 and his father was one of Gallinal's trusted foremen. Today he leads the horserides. If you speak Spanish, you can hear his account of what it was like to live on the estancia under Gallinal in an afternoon tour.

---

20 A series of unsuccessful British attempts to seize control of Spanish-controlled areas of the River Plate during the Napoleonic Wars, when Spain was an ally of Napoleon's France.

21 www.guruguay.com/dieste-rural-schools

The hotel

Nowadays as a country hotel, San Pedro has thirty-one guestrooms in what was the main house and the hostelry where the numerous visitors were hosted, arranged around a central shady quad. The common areas have overstuffed leather sofas and huge fireplaces. A mysterious old library, antique writing-desks and limited internet will get your creative juices flowing. It's an ideal retreat all year round.

Guest rooms—including Dr Gallinal's double—are spacious with antique furniture. A highlight is the bedroom fireplaces which are lit in the winter. The rooms I stayed in had large bathrooms with pedestal sinks, extra-large showers and tons of piping hot water.

The on-site restaurant is run by a well-known chef with all-you-can-eat buffet featuring traditional country dishes and the Mediterranean cuisine beloved by Uruguayans.

Things to do

Relaxing Laze by two outdoor swimming pools. There's a third small heated indoor pool and a tennis court. Take time out at the close of each day to watch the sun set over the River Timote valley.

Horseriding expeditions go out for an hour every morning and afternoon led by Beto. They start around a camp fire. Munch on *tortas fritas* as the horses are saddled.

Seasonal activities Every day there's a menu of activities available at the front desk to plan your day. It almost felt like there was too much to do and that we'd never get to the poolside.

Children's activities San Pedro is magical for children. They can roam completely free. There are expeditions to see lambs and calves (including their births in the spring), egg-collecting and fishing. And there are rabbits and guinea pigs to pet.

Games room Separate from the main hotel, the game room has table-tennis, table football, pool and a large screen TV with comfy sofas. There's an outdoor jungle-gym.

What you should know

There's a deliberate policy to limit Wi-Fi It's only available in the reception and the library.

Activity scheduling can be erratic. Relax, this is South America. If there's an activity you are really interested in, don't get irritated. Talk to manager. He will make things happen.

Experienced staff are hard to come by in such an out-of-the-way location and San Pedro is the department's second largest hotel with lots of roles to fill. When I visited, some areas were not as pristine as you would expect from a hotel of this category. A new manager is turning things around.

What's nearby

The Cerro Colorado bell tower[22] Everyone calls the town closest to San Pedro Cerro Colorado after a now defunct train station. However its official name is Alejandro Gallinal and it was founded by Alberto Gallinal who donated the land to the local townspeople and built the school, the police station, the clinic, an amphitheatre and a very ornate water tower out of his own pocket. Gallinal also built a carillon or bell tower. In 2016, the system was overhauled and now traditional Uruguayan marches, the national anthem and even The Marseillaise ring out on festival days. The tower is illuminated at night—a spectacular thing in the middle of the country and the pride of the town. Climb to the top of the bell tower for spectacular views. The keys are with Leonardo who works in the government office (the Junta Local) at the foot of the building. Ask San Pedro de Timote to call and arrange your visit.

---

22   www.guruguay.com/cerro-colorado

Meet the local wordsmith Roberto Diringuer is a local folklore musician who has shared the stage with some of Uruguay's greats. Nowadays he works at the Cerro Colorado community radio station and has published books on San Pedro and local gaucho, Geronimo Farias. He's currently working on a longer history of the area. He performs regularly at lunch times at the estancia and you'll see him hanging out with Beto. Definitely invite him for a beer if you speak Spanish or can find a translator. Not only is he a delightful person, he is on a personal mission to share the history and legends of deepest Florida.

Getting to San Pedro de Timote

R7 km 142.500 and off-road Montevideo (2 h 30 m) Florida (1 h 30 m) Atlantida (2 h 15 m) Punta del Este (3 h 30 m) Colonia (4 h)

Driving From Montevideo (157 km) take the rambla out of the city, then R5 to Florida, then R56 and then R7 to Cerro Colorado. The highways are reasonable. In Cerro Colorado at the belltower (R7 km142.5) make a sharp left. The last 14 km are unpaved but fine for a regular car. From the airport take the road to Pando and then Ruta 7 to Cerro Colorado. From Atlantida take R11 north to R7 (a very direct drive). From Punta del Este take the panoramic R12 (stop off at Pueblo Edén, see *Beaches, Jose Ignacio, Things to do*) to R7. From Colonia del Sacramento take R1 and R11 to Canelones, R5, R56 and R6. Turn right at R6 km 133.800 and follow the signs. The last kilometres could flood during high rains (double check with the estancia) in which case enter on the R7.

Contact Write to <u>reservas@sanpedrodetimote.com</u>

Estancia Los Platanos, Treinta y Tres

Estancia Los Platanos lies in a remote spot of the rolling sierras of central Uruguay on the border between the rural departments of Treinta y Tres and Florida. The estancia is run by Marina, the sixth-generation owner of Los Platanos, and her husband Andres. Together with their daughters, they welcome a maximum of eight guests who want to leave the twenty-first century behind and work and play on a small working estancia tending cattle and sheep.

Marina's ancestors, the Respeiros, emigrated from France in the 1850s. They built the ranch house around a central well and stone courtyard. The roof tiles still intact today came over by boat from France. For over a century, the estancia served as a general store and a stagecoach post on the Camino Real, the main route from Montevideo to the north-east border with Brazil (nowadays Ruta 7). Both Marina and Andres' great grandparents fought in the civil uprisings of 1897 and 1904 and the family share their history through a small museum in the living room. The tombs of the patriarchs can be seen in the cemetery at nearby Nico-Batlle. The estancia was initially very large but over the generations the land has been divided as family members and loyal employees inherited portions. Marina's grandparents owned almost three thousand acres. Marina and her brother inherited a third each. The other third was left to the grandfather's Afro-Uruguayan foreman who had worked on the estancia from the age of fifteen. He had arrived with the railroad and a fourteen year old wife. Nowadays in his eighties he still lives locally.

The estancia has just three guestrooms. The two courtyard guestrooms are decorated with natural fabrics and weathered wood. The bathrooms are large with elegant fixtures and would not be out of place in a five-star hotel. A family room (sleeps 4) is complete with turned wood bedframes.

Los Platanos offers traditional estancia-style meals—abundant, fresh, and tasty—lovingly prepared by Marina, ably assisted by the rest of the family. Breakfast always includes fresh home-made bread or pastries. Marina, who speaks good English, offers classes in typical Uruguayan country cooking for adults and children. Rainy days call for breadmaking.

I was surprised to see no fans, AC or mosquito nets. Here we are on the sierras and relatively high up. This means—unless the summer has been really rainy—no insects.

Things to do

Experiencing life of a real estancia The family welcomes you to get involved in the daily work of the farm. You need to throw away your watch for a while. If the pressing task of the day is to treat a cow with an injured hoof, then first you'll help Andres catch the full-grown beastie out in the field. Bring her in to the coral. Lasso her in order to lay her down. All this before the treatment can begin. "We don't invent work though," says Andres. "If there's nothing to do, we'll go out riding or trekking."

Abundant wildlife Marina's grandfather banned hunting on the estancia last century and the family still adheres to his wishes. At dawn you can see lots of birds. Around 10 in the morning, armadillos (*mulitas*) are out and about. Mid-afternoon down at the watering hole you may get to see otters sunning themselves. Otters in Uruguay are called *lobitos del rio* which translates as little river wolves. The close of day is probably the most interesting time of day to see wildlife. Birds are returning to their nests. Other animals easy to spot around dusk include foxes (*zorros*), nutria (a type of beaver), *ñandú* (the American ostrich), skunk (*zorrillo*), *hurones* (part of the ferret family) and opposum (*comadrejas*).

What's nearby

Cerro Chato – Triple frontier town where women voted for the first time in South America (R7 km 250) Cerro Chato lies on the dividing lines of three departments—Treinta y Tres, Durazno and Florida. Here, a local may live in one department, send her children to school in another and shop in a third. In 1927 a referendum was called to decide once and for all which department the town should belong to. The Uruguayan feminist movement was strong at the time and the women of Cerro Chato called upon to vote. Political shenanigans meant the result was never declared however the stalemate has had its benefits. This town of three thousand inhabitants has three municipal governments, three budgets and six parliamentary representatives. Visit the house where the first universal vote in South America took place and the monument to the triple frontier. The truncated pyramid of local granite represents the inconclusive result. The spotlight at the centre of the pyramid symbolises the active role of women in the political campaign. At the foot of each set of three steps you are in a different department.

Estación AFE Nico Perez – Ex railway town, José Batlle y Ordóñez (R7 km 204) Nico Perez and José Batlle y Ordóñez are two towns which were once one. A political fallout divided the town literally into two—one side of the road took the name José Batlle y Ordóñez and the other side kept the old name, Nico Perez. At the time of the split Nico Perez was a prosperous town. The railroad had arrived in 1891 and Nico Perez was the terminus, to continue inland passengers had to switch to stagecoach. Being the end of the line, the station has a giant turntable which I saw in use the day I was there. Sadly the railroad in Uruguay stopped running regularly in 1985. Today infrequent trains mainly carrying rice and cattle on their way to Montevideo pass through but do not stop at Nico Perez. This magnificent piece of railway history languishes as a mere backdrop for the birthday photos of Nico-Batlle's Sweet Sixteens.

How to get to Estancia Los Platanos

R7 km 234 Montevideo (4 h) Atlantida, Piriapolis, La Paloma, Punta del Diablo, Tacuarembó (4-5 h)

Estancia Los Platanos is close to the town of Valentines on Ruta 7. R7 after Illescas is poor, has a few unexpected curves and lots of potholes. Drive with care.

Driving From Montevideo, the simplest route is to take Ruta 5 to Florida, then Ruta 56 to Ruta 7. Drive along Ruta 7 till the 234 km marker. Turn right and the entrance to the estancia is right there. From the airport, take Ruta 101 to Ruta 8 till Ruta 11 to Ruta 7. From Atlantida take R11 north to R7. From beaches in Maldonado, a route that keeps to mainly paved highways is R9, turn right onto R8, then left onto R80 through Migues to R7. From Punta del Diablo, take R14 to R7 (R14 to Varela is mostly unpaved). From Tacuarembó take R26 to Ramon Trigo, cut across to Fraile Muerto and then down the R7.

Bus From Montevideo there are five buses daily to Valentines. Check out the bus timetable for buses to Cerro Chato. The family will pick you up from the road (they can see you descending).

Airport transfer Have Andres pick you up at the airport in the family's roomy 4×4. As he knows the highway like the back of his hand, you can be safely in Los Platanos an astonishing two hours after touch-down. For up to 4 people, the cost is 100 USD one way—an absolute bargain.

Contact Write to Marina at marina@estancialosplatanos.com or visit www.estancialosplatanos.com

GURU'GUAY

Horsey treats!

To get a discount don't forget to tell the estancia the Guru told you about them!!

Estancia Yvytu Itaty, Tacuarembó

Pedro and Nahir moved to Yvytu Itaty a quarter of a century ago though they have always worked land in the area. The estancia is on the Haedo highlands in north-central Uruguay. It's frequently windy and the ground rocky. The name Yvytu Itaty (pronounced ee-vee-TOO ee-ta-TEE) are two Guaraní words meaning wind and stony land. Any farm under a thousand hectares in this part of Uruguay needs to have a second income to simply make ends meet. So the couple who were struggling as full-time farmers decided to supplement their income by inviting tourists into their home.

Activities involve taking part in what is going on on the estancia and horseriding. If the weather is good you can go out twice a day on horse-back. Experienced riders are welcome to saddle up and take off alone. The Arroyo Malo borders the estancia and makes for great swimming in summer time. The solitude is as immense as the horizon. You actually hear the sound of the wind rush through the feathers of enormous birds of prey soaring overhead. Be prepared to be startled by the almost mechanical whirring of pheasants taking off at high speed when you're almost on top of them.

The estancia has two guest rooms—a double with an en-suite bathroom and a room for up to four—which are charming though a little spartan.

Nahir cooks four meals a day for guests. It's simple estancia food—roasted meat, lots of stews—though she is happy to cater to vegetarians, celiacs, etc. with advance notice. Even in winter fresh salads were part of the meal, which is not the case in all estancias. Portions are enormous. You are served your first plateful but after that you're expected to go up to the stove and help yourself.

Part of the warmth at Yvytu Itaty inevitably comes from Nahir and Pedro's glowing hospitality. It's remarkable when you consider that they speak very little English—though I suspect Nahir knows much more than she lets on. Where there's a will there's a way, as they say. But get ready to exercise even your very limited Spanish.

One of my most magical moment was milking a cow in the morning to the strains of a tango orchestra on the radio (we are in Uruguay after all) while a sheepdog puppy gambolled around the milking stool. The other was flicking through the family photo album with Nahir as she showed me photos of her family parading on horseback in the Patria Gaucha—a major gaucho festival—each year. That was when I understood why a Londoner had taken a transatlantic flight just to stay at this ranch for ten days. And returned several years later. This is a chance to inhabit an alternative reality.

What you should know

The estancia is in a remote area The final ten miles are on a grass track. You can definitely drive a regular car there but stick to the track.

There is no electricity this far from civilisation and internet is only available in the evening when a generator is turned on for a couple of hours. Obviously there's no TV.

Accommodation is back to basics Water is from a spring. A salamander is fired up to heat water for your shower. I went in winter and though it was cold the hot meals taken in the kitchen with its wood-burning stove, or in front of the roaring fire in the living room, plus a pile of blankets for my bed were enough to keep me cosy.

If it rains there's not much to do Bring some good books and comfortable pyjamas and slippers. Nahir told me of a couple whose stay coincided with three days of solid rain. They spent the entire time in their pyjamas in front of the fire and loved absolutely every minute. Even if it rains the work goes on, and Pedro will be out in the thick of it. Just make it known if you want to join him.

This is the most accessibly priced estancia You will not get a cheaper ranch stay than at Yvytu Itaty. The all-inclusive rate is 2200 pesos per person in a double.

What's nearby

San Gregorio de Polanco - muralled town on a vast lake Two hours from Tacuarembó lies this little town, almost an island in its isolation on the edge of a huge lake. When I was living in Buenos Aires in the early 90s, word got out of a tiny rural town that had become a living open-air art gallery in deepest Uruguay. The murals survive and many have been repainted. Walk or cycle around the quiet streets to see what you stumble upon and enjoy the white, sandy beaches surrounded by pine forests. Stay at the incongruously named Hotel Bali.

How to get to Estancia Yvytu Itaty

R5 km 352.800, off-road Montevideo (5 h), Paysandú (4 h), Carmelo (6 h), Flores (4 h)

Driving From Montevideo take Ruta 5. At the 352.800 km marker (50 km before the city of Tacuarembó) turn left and drive 12 km along grass tracks. At the signpost turn left and drive 3 km until you get to the entrance (5 h). From Paysandú (220 km) take R26. Take the turn-off to Tambores. Drive through the town and then 17 km until you reach a Yvytu Itaty signpost. Turn right and drive 3 km to the entrance. R26 is in poor condition. Fill your tank beforehand as there are no gas stations on the highway.

Bus From Montevideo buses (Agencia Central, Nuñez, Turil and Corporacion) leave every hour or so. From Paysandú buses (Agencia Central, Chadre, Nuñez and COPAY) leave every two hours. From Buenos Aires Nossar travels three days a week overnight. From Brazil, TURIL travels twice a week from Porto Alegre (7 h 30 m) and from Florianopolis via Porto Alegre between December and March. International buses should be booked well in advance.

Tacuarembó bus station transfer It takes an hour from the bus station to the estancia. Pedro will pick you up at the bus station (1700 pesos round trip in 2017).

Contact Write to Nahir at yvytuitaty@hotmail.com

Estancia La Paz, Paysandú

Taking advantage of a slump in land prices after the Uruguayan Great Civil War (1839-1851) a British immigrant, Richard Bannister Hughes purchased La Paz, some of the best agricultural land in western Uruguay in 1856. Hughes was a trailblazer. He imported Durham cows which improved cattle stock nationally and the first mechanical wheat harvester from the USA. At the entrance to La Paz you can still see the metal fence-posts—stamped 'Liverpool'—which he brought over in the 1860s to replace stone corrals. The introduction of fencing ushered Uruguayan agriculture into a period of unparalleled prosperity as livestock could be better cared-for, organised and breeds improved. The estancia is built entirely of materials brought from the UK.

Anne Wyaux's parents arrived in Uruguay from Belgium almost a century later. After six years of sacrifice as immigrants in a new land, with savings and a loan from friends, they bought La Paz which had fallen into wrack and ruin in 1960. Anne, the owner of La Paz, recalls sleeping under the outside verandah to escape the bats and the leaks inside the house. The estancia eventually became profitable after Pierre Wyaux travelled to France and brought back a new breed of cow, the Charolais. A very pretty white cow, it produced the leaner beef that was in demand in European markets. La Paz still breeds around seven hundred award-winning Charolais, Angus and Hereford on 1800 hectares (almost 4500 acres).

There are seven rooms at La Paz, two of them suites for up to four. Furniture includes huge beds including one inherited from Anne's great-grandparents in Belgium. Décor is chintzy, country style though bathrooms are elegant and modern. Meals—standard Uruguayan fare like a tasty steak, a cheesy pasta—are served in what was originally the general store or *pulpería* where the gauchos collected and spent their wages. The grounds include a small swimming pool (open from October) with a sun-deck and a tennis court. For a small extra cost, you can reserve the spa with jacuzzi and/or sauna, or request a massage. Take leisurely bike rides and be sure to check out the little church on site which was loving restored by Anne's father.

What you should know

Riding is not included in the regular tariff Rather than a ranch holiday, La Paz offers a relaxing country retreat .

Don't reserve full board This is the only estancia with a truly unique restaurant 30 minutes away.

Where to eat

La Pulpería, Casa Blanca

Thirty minutes drive from La Paz lies Casa Blanca, a colourful village perched on the banks of the River Uruguay. A stone's throw across the river lies Argentina. Casa Blanca has been the site of meat-packing for over two hundred years. It was the birthplace of 'Paysandú ox tongue', a high-status canned food imported to the UK in the 1800s as "a delicious delicacy for breakfast, luncheon or supper ... very suitable for picnics, yachting, etc". There's just one employer in this town of five hundred souls and that's the meat-packer which provides funds for the local clinic, a small art cinema, and in the last few years an eccentric, top-quality, non-profit restaurant.

The restaurant is in a former general store. With its gorgeous brickwork, soaring arched ceilings, stained glass and a very rare vertical harpsichord (one of just five clavicytheria in the world), the dining room has a mini-cathedral feel. All produce is either grown on site—the artichokes, the mushrooms, the strawberries—or procured locally—the wine and the fish—and the meat of course is all top-notch and aged. You'll be greeted with a glass of complementary house champagne. Menu items (all in Spanish, take your dictionary) have prosaic names like Faun's Sperm. Recommended dishes include the fish soup (*sopa de pescado*) and the aged beef with mushrooms (*bife ancho con setas*).

Have you ever dreamed of eating in a restaurant where you could order extra dishes on the house—just to taste—if you couldn't make up your mind? It exists and it's here in the Uruguayan outback. You can even solicit use of a simple cabin if you need to sleep off a few glasses of wine before hitting the road.

Visit La Pulpería and live like a *caudillo*[23] for a few hours. The menu is fixed price—a remarkable 1300 pesos for four courses including a coffee menu. Open daily noon-10.30pm closed Tuesdays. La Pulpería recommends taking Independencia street south 11 km from the centre of Paysandú. In Casa Blanca turn right and go past the church to the end of the street. Reservations are essential via lapulperia@fricasa.com.uy

What's nearby

The historic Anglo meat packers (Ex Frigorífico Anglo), Fray Bentos Uruguay's second UNESCO heritage site is unexpected. The Anglo revolutionised food processing in the twentieth century. The factory was opened in 1859 by the German inventors of the Oxo cube and fed the country's troops during World War One. In 1924 the British took over and began exporting frozen beef. Fray Bentos meat pies and Oxo cubes are still popular brands in the UK. At its peak the factory employed 4,000 people to slaughter 6,000 animals a day. Who visits an old meat factory on holiday, right? But actually it's fascinating. The factory is so perfectly preserved it's like a ghost town. Perhaps because there's so little signage in English it's as if the book keepers and butchers just upped and left. There are some excellent English speaking guides. This may be the historical highlight of your trip. Go straight through the town to the river, then turn left. El Anglo is the district as well as the factory. Open daily 9am-5pm closed Mondays

---

23 Latin American strong man or lord of the manor

How to get to Estancia La Paz

R3 km 336 and off-road Montevideo (4 h 30 m) Paysandú (40 m) Fray Bentos (1 h) Carmelo (3 h) Flores (2 h) Tacuarembó (4 h). La Paz is located between R24 and R3.

From Montevideo Take Ruta 1 out of Montevideo and then Ruta 3 till the signposted turn-off at km 336 then 12 km of dirt road. **Break the journey** with a stop at Estancia La Estiria in Flores (R3 km 209.3). A day package includes lunch, horseriding, swimming, hammocks for siestas and more for just 1100 pesos per person. You'll be grateful you took the break, particularly on a hot summer's day. See *Estancias, La Estiria.*

Buses (Agencia Central, Chadre, Nuñez and COPAY) leave apx. every two hours for Paysandú.

From Carmelo 3 hours via Fray Bentos. From Fray Bentos it's a one hour drive on the R24 (there are plans to pave it). Buses (just two per day) take five hours.

From Tacuarembó Take Ruta 26 from Tacuarembó. At the time of writing it is very potholed though there are rumours it will be resurfaced in 2018. For now calculate 4 hours to drive the 200+ km though an experienced driver can do it in 2.5 hours. Buses (COPAY and Alonso) take 3.5 hours.

From Argentina by bus There is a direct overnight bus (Flechabus) from Buenos Aires to Paysandú. The city across the river in Argentina is Colón. COPAY runs from Colón to Paysandú twice daily (45 mins).

Contact Write to contacto@estancialapaz.com.uy or visit www.estancialapaz.com.uy

STOP PRESS At time of printing we were informed that La Paz has been put on the market. We really hope this historic estancia will continue to serve travellers. Visit the Guru'Guay site for updates[24].

---

24 www.guruguay.com/uruguay-guide-updates

Estancia La Estiria, Flores

La Estiria was settled almost a hundred years ago by an Austrian couple who had inherited land in Flores, the smallest department in Uruguay. Estiria is the Spanish word for Steiermark, the southern state in Austria where the couple originated.

Today the 2200-hectare estancia (almost 5500 acres) is still a working ranch with a thousand mainly black Angus cows and eight hundred sheep. The estancia is still run by the family. Gunther, great grandson of the first owners, and his wife Araceli speak excellent English, French and German and are there on weekends. During the week, you'll be looked after by the staff—Natalia (who speaks English), Maria who provides the home-cooked meals and Leonardo the gaucho. The staff are outstanding hosts who gave me some handy horseriding tips.

La Estiria has twelve guestrooms—the suites are in the main estancia building with antique furniture brought over from Austria. The décor is elegant yet homely with its open fireplaces, creaking wooden staircases, a lace-covered piano and sepia family photos of Austria. Guestrooms in the outer buildings are more plainly decorated with little wood-burning stoves. They're ideal for summer as they look out onto the pool area. The swimming pool is a highlight. Under the trees it's an attractive T-shape and a reasonable size for swimming. The area is surrounded by sunbeds and the pool though unheated is ready to use all year round.

The estancia stretches over vast flat fields for almost as far as the eye can see. Though the terrain is not adventurous for riding there are various trails to cover.

The estancia is self-sufficient and you'll be served what is grown and raised on site. We went out egg collecting before dark. Food was very fresh and very tasty. Maria bakes daily. There's hot tea and coffee available all day in the living room which is a nice touch as most accommodation does not provide tea-making facilities.

For children this is an enchanted house, what with the wooden staircases, the gabled Austrian-style rooms, the huge stables, a giant chess set, the pool and the wild and domestic animals on site including capibaras and deer so tame they nuzzle you.

La Estiria makes a great pit-stop on the R3 between Montevideo and Paysandú They offer a day package which includes lunch, swimming and high tea. You'll definitely want to fit in a siesta after lunch under the trees. There's access to a nice-sized, well-thought out changing room with a shower. The Day Package is just 1100 pesos per person and includes two meals, access to all the activities of the estancia including horseriding and children's activities and unlimited tea and coffee.

How to get to Estancia La Estiria

R3 km 209.3 Montevideo (2 h 30 m) Colonia (3 h) Carmelo (2 h 30 m) Paysandú (2 h)

Driving From Montevideo take R1 and then R3 to just after km 209. The estancia entrance is on the left and visible from the road. Ruta 3 is in excellent condition. From Paysandú, take R3 until the entrance (2 hrs). Couldn't be simpler. From Carmelo, take R21 to R57 to R3. From Colonia del Sacramento take R1 to Rosario, R2 to Cardona, R57 to R3.

Bus From Montevideo buses (Nuñez and COPAY) leave apx. every two hours (3 h). Buy a ticket to Trinidad though you will get off after. Bus drivers know where to drop you off. The estancia is 2 km from the entrance and they will come and pick you up. The same companies travel from Paysandú.

Contact Write to Araceli at contacto@laestiria.com or visit www.laestiria.com

Caballos de Luz, Rocha

Less than an hour from Rocha's wildest beaches, nestling in a rocky mountain range of native forest, verdant pasture and pristine creeks, lovers of horses and foodies will find your country paradise.

The owners—Lucie who is originally from Austria and her Uruguayan husband Santiago—and their colleagues are real horse enthusiasts who consider their horses their partners, not their property. They train using natural horsemanship techniques without force or violence and can talk about the personalities and origins of their horses for hours.

Caballos de Luz offers riding for adventure lovers, not placid treks. Their guided trails cover wildly different terrain—hills, thickets and rivers. A regular horse-ride takes anything from two to four hours depending on your interest and ability. Beginners receive classes in the paddock before heading out. This was the most varied riding I experienced and ended with an incredible sunset from the top of the sierras and cantering back after dark.

Cuisine is also a big part of the Caballos de Luz experience. Lucie and Santiago are well-travelled and they love to cook creative meals inspired by Thai, Indian and Mexican cuisine. Finally, spices! Most of the vegetables are from their own organic garden and they use milk products and honey from the neighbours' organic farm. The meals are so delicious even as a fervent carnivore I was completely sold.

Accommodation is rustic. This is not a four-star hotel, it's a million-star hotel, says Lucie. Each room has stunning views and a deck for sun bathing and star gazing. The most conventional room is an en suite double with private terrace overlooking the valley and mountains. Out overlooking the sierra is the two-person geometric wood-panelled Dome with its own wood-burning stove, perfect for honeymooners. Families can choose The Cottage, a thatched-roof cabin next to the paddock which sleeps 2-4.

Things to do

Relax and enjoy the silence As half of your day will be taken with riding, the other half is your time to do with as you wish. There are lots of books to read, hammocks to swing in and a piano. Some people like to help out in the kitchen garden. Lucie says that most people come to ride and spend the rest of their time sleeping. And of course you don't need to ride at all if you are just looking for serenity and silence.

Swim A creek is just a three-minute walk away and makes summer super agreeable.

Sustainable living projects and alternative building styles Caballos de Luz is part of a loose community of thirty or so families who have chosen to move to the sierras over the last decade. They are like-minded souls living self-sufficiently in harmony with nature. Most of the houses are self-built and there are three organic farms. Lucie is happy to call ahead and set up visits for you. Quite a few people speak English, so you'll have more access to local information than you might in other parts of Uruguay. Rides with children will stop off at one of the local farms to visit the animals.

Massage and yoga The community includes a Thai-style masseuse, a yoga instructor and a certified osteopath. Music and meditation take place occasionally in the curious grass-roofed dome in the middle of the valley. If you are interested in any of this, ask Lucie what is available during your stay.

Dedicated horseriding treks Lucie loves to arrange 2-10 day treks for three people or more alternating nights camping by the fire with lodging in simple country homes. This horseriding experience takes you far off from the beaten track and into Uruguay's real back country.

What you should know

This is not an estancia There are no cows and sheep but if you are a horse-lover this is the place for you.

There's no Wi-Fi and there is no plan to install a connection. The house runs on solar power so there's no air-conditioning or central heating.

Recognising that everyone's different first thing in the morning breakfast is totally self-service and private. After dinner, you head back to your room with provisions—eggs, nutty bread to toast, butter, salt, oil—to make yourself a delicious breakfast. There's good coffee and an espresso pot in your room and a little camping stove. Next morning, sitting out on your secluded terrace looking out over the valley with nothing but the sounds of the river, the birds and your eggs sizzling, you'll not imagine a better breakfast.

Riding in the rain Rides go ahead in the rain but not when there are storms or high winds because the horses become difficult to handle. If the weather is too stormy to ride you'll receive a discount.

For larger groups the dome and the cabin can fit in two more people.

What's nearby

See *Beaches, La Paloma* One hour drive away

How to get to Caballos de Luz

R109 and off-road Montevideo (3 h 30 m) La Paloma (1 h) Jose Ignacio (1 h 30 m) Punta del Diablo (2 h)

Driving The inn is north of the city of Rocha (Ruta 9 km 209). Head straight through town to R109. After 10 km turn right at the sign to Camino de las Sierras and Caballos de Luz. After 3.1 km you will reach the entrance.

Bus Take a bus to the town of Rocha (note, Rocha has virtually nothing of interest to the traveller). COT, CYNSA and Rutas del Sol run from Montevideo to Rocha daily (3 hours depending on stops). There are also good regional connections from other departments.

Bus station transfer The inn is apx. 15 km north of Rocha. Lucie and Santiago can pick you up for a 20 USD fee. A taxi costs 25 USD.

Contact Write to Lucie at caballosdeluz@gmail.com or visit www.caballosdeluz.com

The Guru's final analysis

You've read all about each estancia. Now to make your decision a little easier....

	San Pedro T.	La Paz	La Estiria	Los Platanos	El Ceibo	Yvytu Itaty	Caballos de Luz
Working ranch		X	X	X	X	X	
Country hotel	X	X	X				
Daily horse-rides included in rate	X		X	X	X	X	X
Swimming pool or river a minute from room[25]	X	X	X				X
Traditional ranch food	X	X	X	X	X	X	
Exclusively vegetarian meals							X
Restaurant with buffet[26]	X						
Air conditioning	X	X	X		X		
Owner or member of staff speaks good English	X[27]		X	X	X		X
Unusually few insects in summer				X			
Facilities especially for children	X		X				
Capacity to host your wedding	X	X	X		X		
Number of guestrooms	31	7	12	3	5	2	3
Hours drive from Montevideo and/or airport[28]	3	4.5	2.5	4	1	5	3.5

25 All estancias have places to swim on site so we mention those that are right next to the ranch house.
26 At the other estancias you will generally be asked a few hours earlier to choose from two main course options.
27 At the time of writing San Pedro has taken on bilingual receptionists.
28   If you hire a transfer with the estancia travel time will be significantly shorter given they know the roads very well.

Wine Country

Uruguay is on the same southern parallel—between 30° and 35°—as the best wine-producing regions of Argentina, Australia, Chile and South Africa. However our climate is completely different to the dry, dry wine-growing areas of Argentina and Chile high in the Andes foothills almost a thousand miles away. Uruguay lies low—its highest point is just 1685 ft (514 m) above sea level—and is surrounded by water—immense rivers to the south and west and the Atlantic Ocean to the east. Uruguay is windy, damp, oceanic and cool for South America. It has more in common with Bordeaux (France) than it does with Argentina or Chile.

Tannat – The signature Uruguayan wine

Wine-making began in Uruguay in the mid-seventeenth century. Vines were brought from Spain and people made their own wine at home. The first person to see wine production as a business opportunity was a Basque immigrant, Pascual Harriague. He planted a number of different varieties in 1870 in search of a varietal that would adapt well to Uruguay's soil and climate. The wine that proved most popular with his clients was a Tannat, a variety of French origin. In fact locals went crazy for Tannat. Harriague was awarded a national prize and less than a decade later, Tannat was so ubiquitous it had become THE wine consumed by Uruguayan citizens. Today one in every three bottles of wine produced in Uruguay is a Tannat.

Tannat is a full-bodied red wine with dark fruit and spice aromas and flavours. It goes wonderfully well with beef and lamb, pasta and strong cheeses. It's also incredibly varied: "The styles of single-variety Uruguayan Tannat vary like the styles of Syrah in France," says wine writer W Blake Gray[29]. "There's Tannat that's tannic like tarbrush and fresh like cherry juice."

---

29 blog.wblakegray.com/2013/04/what-uruguayan-tannat-tastes-like.html

Tannat is full of tannins, which lower blood pressure and cholesterol and has been declared the world's healthiest wine. However those tannins need a good wine-maker to tame them. Thirty or forty years ago they roamed unfettered. That's no longer the case. Wine-making has been professionalised under a new generation of local enologists getting their wine-making credentials in Uruguay and specialising abroad.

But when you come to Uruguay don't just stick with Tannat. Uruguay is producing great wines in all categories. Try the Albariño, Cabernet Franc, Cabernet Sauvignon, Merlot, Sauvignon Blanc, Tempranillo and Viognier, to name just a few.

Wine regions

Wine is produced in fifteen of Uruguay's nineteen provinces however there are three wine regions that are best set up to receive visitors.

Montevideo and Canelones
Most of Uruguay's wine is produced in vineyards within a 30-mile (50 km) radius of the capital Montevideo and its neighbouring department Canelones. Many are small family-run concerns that have been around for generations whilst some of the big hitters with more than one vineyard will have their principal vineyard in Canelones.
Drive time: 15-60 mins from Montevideo

Carmelo (western Uruguay)
Wineries in Carmelo are almost all dedicated to boutique production in a setting the New York Times called "the Uruguayan Tuscany". Carmelo lies in the department of Colonia, known for UNESCO heritage site, Colonia del Sacramento.
Drive time: 3 h from Montevideo; 1 h from Colonia

Maldonado (south-eastern Uruguay)
Maldonado with its coastal breezes and cooler temperatures has become the new hot spot for Uruguayan wines and may very well be its future. On the way to Maldonado from Montevideo you'll pass Atlantida, a small wine region technically in Canelones but sharing the same climatic characteristics as Maldonado.
Drive time: 45-75 mins from Montevideo; 30 min from Punta del Este.

What to expect

After consultation with local wine experts, Guru'Guay visited ten vineyards in the country's three most productive wine regions. Each vineyard is very different one from the other but what they all have in common is that they produce great wine and they love to show visitors around.

Visits are generally a very personalised experience. You can spend up to three hours at the winery between the tour and the tasting. Tasting usually includes a generous *picada* (a platter of cold cuts and/or cheese) and bread.   Servings will be generous and include reserve wines and barrel tastings. And what really makes the difference, you'll be taken around by a winery principal—the wine-maker or the owner. So plan to visit just one, maximum two wineries in a day.

GURU'GUAY

Share the love!

Tell the winery
you found about them
from Guru'Guay
at the time of booking

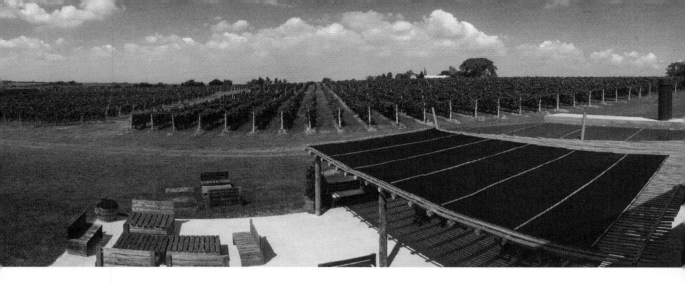

Montevideo & Canelones

Because half the population of Uruguay lives in Montevideo perhaps it was originally for practical reasons that most vineyards were originally planted within thirty miles of the capital. The prime agricultural land of the departments of Montevideo and neighbouring Canelones have rich clay-heavy soils and very gently rolling plains. The River Plate is so wide at this point, the riverbank opposite is 150 miles (250 km) away. Humidity is high and occasionally so is the rainfall. Tannat withstands all of this producing consistently great quality wine. Other varieties include Albariño, Cabernet Sauvignon, Chardonnay, Merlot, Pinot Noir, Sauvignon Blanc and Viognier.

The scale of wineries in the Montevideo-Canelones varies widely. We'll look at four in detail. And if you don't have a chance to get out to a winery while you're in Montevideo, I have included a great little wine bar at the port market to visit which stocks many of the wines mentioned in this book.

The big names

OK, Uruguay's wine production is tiny compared to Argentina's but there are some big brands (on a Uruguayan scale) in Canelones. **Juanicó** is probably one of the five best vineyards in the country and produces a broad portfolio of wines including the ubiquitous Don Pascual. If a Uruguayan wants to take a good wine to a party, they'll choose a Don Pascual. They are enormously professional while managing to keep the personal touch in their tours.

Boutique and family-run

Most Uruguayan wineries are family concerns and many of the wine-makers you meet will be fourth-generation producers. **Artesana** breaks with tradition in that it is first-generation and run by three women. **Pizzorno** is run by the fourth generation of a Catalan family committed to experimentation and innovation. The fourth-generation owners of **Moizo** offer unusual wine-tasting events.

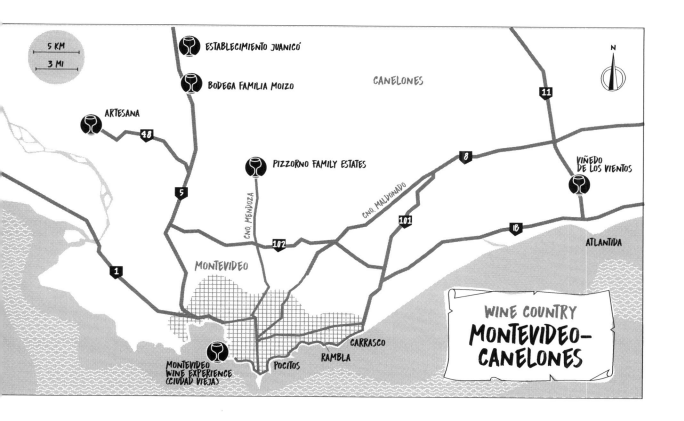

Artesana

A short drive from Montevideo close to a picturesque protected wetlands region, lies Artesana, a new boutique winery run by Analia Lazaneo and Valentina Gatti. Artesana is leading the vanguard of a new generation of wine-makers in Uruguay, many of whom are women (Artesana is the Spanish word for craftswoman).

Artesana is an easy forty-minute drive from Montevideo on the highway and then through countryside lined with pampas grasses and the occasional roadside shrine. The nearest village is enigmatically called Las Brujas, The Witches. The vineyard is on a sloping nine hectares (just over 20 acres) which borders the Santa Lucia river. The land was planted in 2007 and the winery built four years later in time for the first harvest. Right from the start, owner Californian Leslie Fellows had her eye on the international market and Artesana's very first wines were exported to the US. You can find Artesana wines in select shops and restaurants in the USA, Brazil, Canada and the UK.

The vineyard produces 30,000 bottles per year with an eventual plan to produce 50,000. In 2017, Artesana produced Tannat and Merlot and they were Uruguay's only producer of Zinfandel, a red that's very popular in California. According to Artesana, their Zinfandel is more elegant and fresh than the Californian, due to Uruguay's more temperate climate.

Artesana's cuisine stands out

The picada at Artesana was very adventurous. It included an extra-chunky pork pate made with lashings of Tannat Rosado, a pungent goats' cheese, zesty marinaded vegetables (*escabeche*) and *huesito caracú*—grilled bone marrow. A whole beef bone is cut length-wise, seasoned and grilled till the marrow is crunchy on top and bubbling and velvety below. I had never seen this uber-gaucho dish served at a restaurant before. The chef Martin Amengual told us you either love it or hate it. Personally I loved it.

Martin previously worked at Punta del Este's most famous casino hotel. Here he specialises in the classic Uruguayan *parrilla* or grill. Lunch was creative, delicious and good value. Our ultra-lean beef (*entraña*) was accompanied by three types of puré—pumpkin with fire-toasted corn, sweet potato mash with chorizo bites and mashed potato with leek—all toasted on a griddle resting on the *parrilla* embers. Vegetarian options are available.

Wine-tasting

Wine-tasting includes three generous pours of Tannat, Zinfandel and Tannat Rosado and two reserves and a gourmet *picada*. 750 pesos. Wine-tasting plus three-course lunch. 1600 pesos.

Tours from 11am till 4pm from Monday to Saturday. Sunday visits can also be arranged. Email Valentina at turismo@artesanawinery.com and mention dietary restrictions.

How to get to Artesana

Ruta 48 km 3.600

Artesana is a 40-minute drive from downtown Montevideo. Ignore the GPS and do not drive through the city. Instead get to the rambla as quickly as possible and then follow it west until you hit the R5. Take R5 and then left onto R48. Ruta 48 has lots of bends. Follow it till you get to a fork in the road. Artesana is just down on the left.

Establecimiento Juanicó

Juanicó is one of Uruguay's largest wineries employing a hundred people, with vineyards in four different regions of Uruguay and France. Various wine-makers told me that they had heard that despite its size, Juanicó was providing really boutique experiences to visitors. That combined with the fact that the location is stunning and that Juanicó has constantly pushed the vanguard in wine production were excellent reasons to visit.

When the current owners, the Deicas family, bought the winery in 1979 it had long been on the map for innovation—Don Francisco Juanicó having broken with traditional farming techniques in 1830 to build the underground cellar still used today. The Deicas were the first to commission a study of the terroir which revealed the region had the same characteristics as Bordeaux. They embarked on an ambitious renovation and by the 1990s had became the first Uruguayan winery to export abroad and to win a gold medal in Europe. Today their Don Pascual line sells more than any other Uruguayan wine in the world.

Two-thirds of all production is Tannat. But they also produce Chardonnay, Sauvignon Blanc and Gris and Viognier and Cabernet Franc, Cabernet Sauvignon, Merlot, Petit Verdot, Pinot Noir and Shiraz. Juanicó has three wine brands—Don Pascual, Familia Deicas—wines produced in a sole vineyard—and Atlántico Sur, young wines.

The tasting room is grand with pristine white linen, leather sofas and a huge fireplace. The 'Menu with character' includes a unique bonus—you get to choose a bottle of wine from the owner's cellar to drink with your meal. Absolutely any bottle. My guide, a charismatic young Brazilian enologist with great English, waxed on the vintage of my 2000 Tannat. LOVE IT.

Given the spectacular location, guide and wines I confess the meal was a bit of a let-down (soggy pastry, undercooked potatoes). Perhaps it was because I was the only person there. Juanicó receives cruiseship groups in summer so if you prefer a more personal experience, request not to coincide. Though if you do, perhaps the food improves?

Wine-tasting

There are two tastings options. The Don Pascual tasting called 'Pure Character' includes four wines including a reserve, a limited edition and appetisers. 30 USD. The Premium Select tasting includes their five top wines—including an Atlántico Sur single vineyard, Preludio (the first grand cru made in Uruguay), Massimo Deicas Tannat and Licor de Tannat (similar to port, another first) with appetisers. 60 USD. Tours daily 10am and 3pm, Sundays 10am only.

How to get to Juanicó Ruta 5 km 38.200. It's just about impossible to get lost as the vineyard is just off Ruta 5 two blocks after the 38 km road marker coming from Montevideo.

Contact www.juanico.com.uy

Bodega Familia Moizo

Thirty minutes from Montevideo, Moizo is a small vineyard attended by husband and wife team, Omar and Sonia and their three daughters. Omar's paternal great-grandfather came from Piedmont and his mother's ancestors from Trieste in Italy. Omar's grandfather started the winery in 1954. Grandpa Moizo sold table wine to general stores in the interior—the winery still continues to serve those clients out of a sense of tradition and loyalty. However nowadays their focus is on the 50,000 litres of fine wine they produce per year. Wines and blends include Chardonnay, Cabernet Franc Rosé, Merlot, Cabernet Sauvignon and of course Tannat.

The winery is built of rough-hewn stone covered in climbing vines and surrounded by impressive oak trees. The Moizo family's Italian heritage shines through their enthusiastic embrace of the numerous festivals to celebrate the different stages of the wine-making process. At harvest time they hold grape-treading competitions to Italian music.

Wine-tastings

Your tasting will take place in what was originally Omar's grandmother's kitchen. Four generous pours including one reserve wine, with a *picada* and home-made *empanadas*. 30 USD. Omar, who speaks perfect English, will encourage you to let him know which wines you would like to taste—a terrific liberty rarely found in a vineyard—as you browse their shop. So if you are a white wine fan, or if you'd prefer to go with reserve wines, just make your preferences known.

Wine-tasting by the light of the moon

Another thing that makes Moizo unique is the couple's interest in spiritual arts. As well as enologists, they are trained reiki healers and yoga practitioners. Check out the lunar calendar for your visit. If the full moon coincides with any weekend (Friday through Sunday), the family offers guided meditations (in Spanish but it's all about the ambiance, right?) under the full moon. They also offer sunset yoga sessions amongst the vines. Followed by wine-tasting of course.

Write to Omar and Sonia at info@bodegamoizo.com

How to get to Moizo

Ruta 5 km 34.200 It's just about impossible to get lost as the vineyard is just off Ruta 5 two blocks after the 34 km road marker coming from Montevideo. It's just before Juanicó. During organised events they lay on transportation from Montevideo's Tres Cruces bus station.

Pizzorno Family Estates

The Pizzorno vineyard is over a hundred years old. Francisco Pizzorno's great-grandfather emigrated from Italy and the concrete wine tanks he built are still in use today. The winery is currently in the hands of father and son, Carlos and Francisco. Grandfather Alberico lives just across the road from the vineyard. A sprightly 94, he puts his good health down to drinking a bottle of fine wine a day.

The current generations consider themselves ambitious and "experimental", growing eleven varietals on 21 hectares (fifty acres). In any one year, they may experiment with up to eight different ways of making wine using traditional and new methods. One wine expert was amazed to see processes described in a book on Champagne production written in 1887 being carried out in Uruguay today. "One man used a machine that looked similar to the machine I saw in the museum at G.H. Mumm to discorge the wine, while another filled the bottle with a similar antique looking machine."[30] Pizzorno also makes ice wine, a type of dessert wine made from grapes left to freeze naturally on the vine. They experiment with the barrels too. Pizzorno mainly uses oak barrels from France and the US—oak is used in wine-making to vary the colour, flavour, tannins and texture of wine—but they are also trying out oak from Poland and Hungary.

Few Uruguayan vineyards are as successful internationally as Pizzorno. They were one of the earliest vineyards to break into the overseas market and have been exporting an exclusive Merlot Tannat to Waitrose, an up-market supermarket chain in the UK for more than two decades now. When Waitrose started stocking Pizzorno, the wine was labelled 'Tannat Merlot'. Tannat is of course little known outside of Uruguay, and even less so in the UK in the 1990s. Thanks to a tip the day Pizzorno changed the labels to say 'Merlot Tannat' the bottles started to fly off the shelves. Today Pizzorno exports to twelve countries. The day I visited they had broken into the Swiss market.

---

30 awinestory.com/2012/04/a-visit-to-pizzorno-winery-in-uruguay.html

Wine-tastings

Tastings include classic, premium and sparkling/sweet tastings. The first three include four generous pours of three wines plus a reserve or blend. The sweet tasting includes three sparkling wines plus Arazá, an ice wine paired with chocolate. 30-40 USD. The expert tasting includes eight wines and barrel tasting. 50 USD. All tastings include typical Uruguayan snacks. A lunch tasting includes a tour, a premium tasting and a four-course meal. 65 USD.

Tours are scheduled daily at 10.30am, 1pm and 3pm for a maximum of eight people. Wine tours are carried out by Carlos, Francisco or Lucio, a sommelier and friend of the family. They all speak excellent English.

Take a wine flight

Pizzorno offers a 40-minute flight in a four-seater airplane over the Canelones and Montevideo countryside spotting vineyards as you go followed by a premium tasting. The experience lasts three 3 hours. 120 USD per person.

Guesthouse in the vineyard

The family have turned their ancestral home into a chic four-room guesthouse. Each room has views of the vineyards and there is an outdoor jacuzzi set amongst the vines.

How to get to Pizzorno

Ruta 32 km 23.5 Don't get lost in the city. Follow the rambla west until you hit the R5. Take R5, turn right on R102 and left on Camino Pedro Mendoza. Pizzorno offers transfers from Montevideo for 30-35 USD per person return trip.

For all enquiries including accommodation and flights contact Francisco at visitas@pizzornowines.com

Montevideo Wine Experience

On the outer perimeter of the infamous Port Market in Montevideo's Old City lies a small wine-bar run by two charming young guys serving exclusively Uruguayan wines. Nico is from an old wine-producing family. Liber was named Uruguay's second-best sommelier in 2015. They speak great English and are passionate that the rest of us get to know Uruguayan wines as intimately as they do.

I first came across them thanks to guests of mine who told me about this wonderful little wine-bar they'd discovered. It seemed to exert a mysterious force on them. Every day they would spend the afternoon hanging out there, and would stagger back not only full of (info about) Uruguayan wine, but local politics, culture, etc. I had to go and check it out and I can confirm, with their great wines, wonderful service and generous conviviality, a traveller's time is well-spent at Montevideo Wine Experience.

Try wine by the glass (from 120 pesos) or a wine-based cocktail. Liber makes a killer caipirinha with Sauvignon Blanc. Accompany your drink choosing from a small menu of tapas. Alternatively you can order from the Port Market next door or amazing fish restaurant Es Mercat and they'll deliver. So you'll never have to leave your stool.

Montevideo Wine Experience offers all their wines by the bottle at supermarket prices to take home.

Rambla 25 de agosto de 1825 244, Ciudad Vieja. Open daily 11.30am-9pm, closed Mondays in low season

Carmelo

Carmelo lies just east of the confluence of the rivers Uruguay and Paraná, the birth place of the River Plate which then flows past Buenos Aires and on to Montevideo and the Atlantic Ocean. The area has fossil-rich calcareous soil which fascinated Darwin during the six months he spent in Uruguay on his famous Beagle exploration. Those fossils and the mineral-packed soil are great for vines. The presence of the rivers tempers the climate so that Carmelo is significantly warmer than Montevideo. Grapes ripen two to three weeks earlier than in the capital and avoid early frosts.

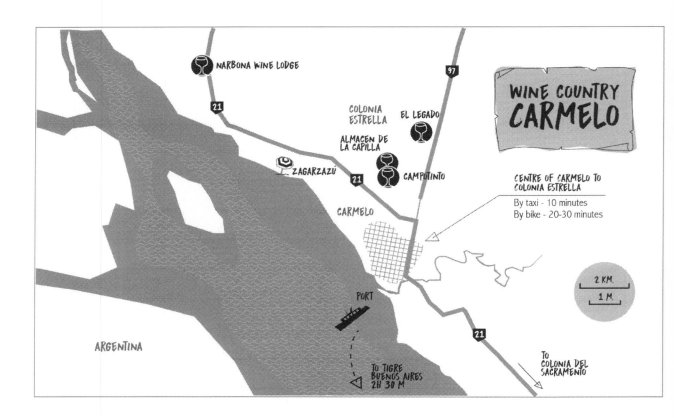

Carmelo is Uruguay's second largest wine-producing area. As well as Tannat, you'll find Cabernet Franc, Cabernet Sauvignon, Chardonnay, Pinot Noir, Sauvignon Blanc, Syrah, Viognier and more. New varietals are being introduced constantly.

Carmelo hosts eight boutique wineries, the largest producing 100,000 bottles of fine wine each year and the smallest just three thousand. The wineries and hotels that are included in this chapter are primarily in the Colonia Estrella neighbourhood which the New York Times baptised "the Uruguayan Tuscany".

Almacén de la Capilla

Flat green fields, dusty brown country roads, squat bushes of lavender and rosemary and a hundred year old general store on the crossroads. A few old guys hanging out chatting, enjoying the early morning sun. This was the scene the day I arrived at Almacén de la Capilla, a 150 year old general store in Colonia Estrella run by fifth-generation wine-maker Ana Paula Cordano.

The oldest vineyard in Carmelo, the Almacén was founded by Antonio Cordano, an immigrant from Genoa, in the 1870s as a general store and a place to meet up with his friends. The store was directly across the road from the San Roque chapel hence the name which means chapel store. Don Antonio planted Criolla vines, a few of which can still be found on site, and produced table wine under the name Bodega Cordano. Fans of former president Jose Mujica (2010-15)—called "the world's 'poorest' president" by the BBC—will be interested to hear that his mother was a Cordano and El Pepe spent some of his childhood summer holidays at the vineyard.

It was Ana Paula's father who moved into fine wine production in the 1970s introducing Tannat, Merlot, Cabernet Franc, Cabernet Sauvignon and Chardonnay among others. Today the vineyard still produces table wine under the Cordano name and fine wines as Almacén de la Capilla under the management of Ana Paula who is the first woman wine-maker at Cordano. She would have liked to have studied enology—the science and study of wine and wine-making—when she graduated from highschool but as an only daughter the idea was inconceivable to her family. It was only when her father passed away—still without having designated a successor—that she decided to follow her dream and run the vineyard herself. Together with her husband Diego they make a great team who will receive you personally.

The Almacén is a lovely place to spend the afternoon with lots of spaces for sitting and enjoying the surrounding countryside. There's Wi-Fi too and a splendid little gift shop. Check out the antique wine presses. During harvest you could have the chance to tread grapes with your bare feet at the Almacén.

Wine-tasting

Tasting includes five wines, a generous *picada*, a traditional dessert and coffee all for 25 USD. Open daily 11am-8pm. Email Ana Paula at almacendelacapilla@adinet.com.uy

How to get to Almacén de la Capilla

Ruta 21 km 257 on the corner of Camino de los Peregrinos and Ana María Carpi de Cordano. The Almacén is a 20-30 minute bike ride from the centre of Carmelo and a ten-minute ride from Zagarzazú beach. Take Ruta 21 out of town, take a left at the roundabout staying on R21. At the 257 km landmark turn right onto a dirt road for just over a mile. It is clearly sign-posted.

CampoTinto

This pretty 24-hectare boutique wine estate (60 acres) complete with a small luxury guesthouse and a restaurant is owned by an Argentine property developer with a passion for wine. At CampoTinto you'll be received personally by the wine-maker Daniel Cis who has set out to produce "the world's best Tannat".

CampoTinto is Carmelo's newest winery opening in 2015, though they'd been producing wine since 2012 at a neighbouring vineyard. They produce around 15,000 bottles a year. Two-thirds are Tannat. In that quest for the best Tannat, CampoTinto is growing Tannat on 24 separate parcels of land. They ferment the harvest from each parcel separately, then after extensive tasting blend to make a Reserve, a Gran Reserve and save the product of the very best plot for their Ícono Tannat.

Carmelo's climate favours whites. CampoTinto are producing a sparkling white made with Moscatel and Trebbiano (CampoTinto calls it by its French name, Ugni Blanc) called *Medio y Medio*—half and half—a classic Uruguayan apertif. *Medio y Medio* can be sickly sweet. Diego assures me that this is a high-range *Medio y Medio*, introduced originally to serve to visitors who had biked into the vineyard during the hottest summer months and wanted something quintessentially Uruguayan yet refreshing to quaff before they hit the Tannat. CampoTinto is also producing a thousand bottles of a delightful Viognier.

Wine-tasting

The wine-tasting includes two Tannat reserve wines, Medio y Medio and barrel tastings. 15 USD. Tasting plus lunch. 55 USD. CampoTinto also provides a gourmet picnic. 65 USD per person. Open Wed-Sun noon-5pm. Reserve with Veronique at info@campotinto.com

How to get to CampoTinto

Follow the directions for the Almacén. CampoTinto is on the road just before.

El Legado

Bernardo Marzuca's father was a businessman and passionate wine-maker. His fortunes were badly affected during a financial crisis in 1982, he fell ill and shortly before he passed away he was forced to sell his beloved 25 hectares (sixty acres) of vines to make ends meet. Years later, in their father's memory, Bernardo and his brother were able to buy back the land. By that time the vines were too old to produce wine-worthy grapes but Bernardo was determined to carry on his father's legacy (*legado* in Spanish). He saved a few of the original vines as a keepsake and imported a small number of Tannat and Syrah plants from France.

He produces just three wines—a Tannat, a Syrah and a blend. Currently he produces just under 5,000 bottles and plans to grow the winery to produce no more than 10,000. The wines are prize-winners and sold primarily sold to visitors though you may be lucky enough to run into a few bottles in a dedicated wine-store or upscale restaurant in Montevideo or Punta del Este.

El Legado is perhaps Uruguay's smallest winery and Bernard and his family tend to every part of the process. They harvest the grapes at night. "It's a real party," he says. Picked at night, the grapes have a temperature of around 60 degrees and they'll only need to cool just a few degrees more for the fermentation process to start. If picked at midday the temperature of the grapes could be 100 degrees. So moonlight harvesting may sound whimsical but it saves time and prevents spoiling.

Wine-tasting

Ample servings of the three wines and barrel servings plus a very generous picada. 25 USD. For groups of eight Bernardo can cook a full-on *asado* (a mighty Uruguayan mixed grill). 50 USD. Email Bernardo bodegalegado@adinet.com.uy

How to get to El Legado

From Carmelo take the R21 and carry on straight across the roundabout at the edge of town. Turn left and follow the signs. There is an easy short-cut along a country back-road between El Legado and the Almacén.

Narbona Wine Lodge

Narbona is the dream winery of Pacha Canton, a charismatic Argentine who has lovingly rebuilt one of Uruguay's oldest vineyards founded in the early 1900s by Frenchman Juan de Narbona. Today's Narbona produces around 80,000-100,000 bottles a year—over half exported to Europe, the USA and Australia. Two-thirds of the fifteen-hectare vineyard (apx. forty acres) is planted with Tannat. Other varieties include Pinot Noir, Petit Verdot, Syrah and Tempranillo.

Narbona's new winery was built in 2009 from limestone quarried from the vineyard. Close to the birthplace of the River Plate, crushed fossils create pockets in the calcareous soil which produce great colour in red wines and wines that age particularly well. The vineyard continues to use the traditional Lyre—or V-shaped—trellis system. Though it takes more advantage of the sun, this system is being phased out in most vineyards (for the three-wire VSP trellis which is less labour-intensive).

Tastings take place in the 1909 wine cellar where the rock ceiling glistens with fossils. The surroundings are sumptuous. At Narbona wine is not a product, it's a ceremony.

There's a luxury hotel on site and guests can shadow wine-maker Valeria Chiola for a day. Valeria comes from a wine-making family in Canelones, has a masters in enology from Italy and she worked in Napa.

Wine-tasting

Narbona offers four tastings per day which includes a tour around the winery, three wines and a *picada* of cheese made at Narbona's own dairy. 50 USD. Pick up a pot of Narbona's own *dulce de leche*, a traditional caramel. It's attracting even more fans in the US than the wines. Email reservas@narbona.com.uy

How to get to Narbona

R21 km 268. Take Route 21 out of town, take a left at the roundabout staying on R21. At the 268 km landmark you will see the lowrise stone buildings and a large sign on the left (ignore the signs to Capilla Narbona a little earlier).

Things to do in Carmelo

Swing bridge The city is known for its bright red rotating bridge which was imported from Germany in 1912. It can be rotated manually by two people to allow tall boats to sail upriver. The bridge takes you out of town. A sign proclaims that anyone who crosses the bridge will always return to Carmelo. You'll be so lucky.

Jose Castro wood sculpture universe (I mean, gallery) Hidden at the back of a hardware store (yes, seriously) through a little door, you'll find a thousand wood carvings of scenes of human desire, suffering, banality and stupidity by Spanish artist Jose Castro. It took my breath away. When I returned to reality and the dusty Carmelo streets an hour later, I realised yet again that these encounters with what feels like parallel universes are what makes time spent in Uruguay unique.

Capilla de San Roque (San Roque Chapel) This mission-style church is an unmistakable landmark in Colonia Estrella. Yellow fever was stalking the land and a number of townspeople left the town for the relative safety of the countryside. They gave thanks by founding the church on August 16 1870. From that time, a mass is held every sixteenth of the month.

There's not a huge amount to do in Carmelo, besides drink wine. Thank god! So that's what you should plan to do. Visit vineyards, drink wine and relax.

Where to stay

The most gorgeous accommodation in Carmelo is located in the vineyards themselves in Colonia Estrella, a ten-minute drive from the centre of Carmelo. As a local said to me: "You have to get as far away from the town centre as you can, to be at the centre of everything." The beauty and peace are priceless.

Just beyond Colonia Estrella lies Zagarzazú, a tiny riverside beach town. Zagarzazú is the nicest beach in Carmelo on the River Uruguay. This village with unpaved roads is a ten-minute bike ride from Colonia Estrella and fifteen minutes from Narbona Wine Lodge. All accommodations below provide free transfers from the city centre which is 4 miles away (6km) and offer guests bicycles. If you are on a budget, stay in the centre of town and bike out to the vineyards in thirty minutes.

Entre Viñas – The cabaña among the vines, Almacén de la Capilla, Colonia Estrella

A romantic wooden cabin for two in the vineyard of wine-makers Cordano. The cabin is a two-minute walk through the vineyards to the Almacén, so it's very private. It has an enormous king-size bed, a very smart bathroom with the trappings of a five star hotel—robes, slippers,—a squashy sofa set in the picture window and a deck overlooking the vines. There's a kitchenette and of course wine glasses and a bottle opener. Breakfast appears magically on the doorstep each morning in a red-checkered picnic basket. Word of warning: despite Diego and Ana Paula's best attempts, they have not been able to provide internet in the cabin, so bring your own or be prepared to head to the store to sit under the vines and send your emails from there. How big a problem is that? Email Ana Paula at almacendelacapilla@adinet.com.uy $$$$

Posada CampoTinto, Colonia Estrella

This charming old farm-house in Colonia Estrella with an interior designed by a top Argentine architect is warm and vibrant. There are four generous-sized suites—two overlooking the gardens and two overlooking the Capilla de San Roque. Eighty percent of CampoTinto guests come to celebrate birthdays and anniversaries and it's easy to see why. There's a pool in rolling gardens reminiscent of Provence where horses graze in the distance. Picnics and wine-tasting can be arranged. On site there's a restaurant with a gorgeous outdoor vine-covered patio serving Uruguayan favourites with gourmet twists without the gourmet prices. Write to Veronique at info@campotinto.com $$$-$$$$

Hotel Puerto Dijama, Zagarzazú beach

Puerto Dijama is a small recently-built hotel with motel-style rooms arranged around a central pool. Dijama's décor is eclectic with the elements of pop-art—including pimped-out antique furniture—combined with restful wood panelling. There's an on-site restaurant open all day with an extensive local wine list and there's a splash pool and jacuzzi. The best thing about Dijama is the manager Pablo who relocated from Rio de Janeiro to Carmelo. Jovial and dynamic, he's can't do enough for guests. The second best thing are the six kayaks available for guests to use on the river. hotelpuertodijama.com $$$-$$$$

Narbona Wine Lodge

Señorita Vino declared Narbona Wine Lodge one the world's three most romantic wineries. The stone building was built in 1909 by Juan de Narbona, a quarry-man who supplied the stone that built Buenos Aires just across the river. However from the 1950s the property fell into disrepair until it was loving restored during the 90s. Nowadays it houses Uruguay's only Relais & Chateaux hotel. There are just five guestrooms. The largest two are huge, each almost 500 square feet. The lounge and restaurant are just as exquisite. There's a small pool with a view of the vineyards. I've had a bunch of guests do their romantic splurge stay at Narbona and everyone has sworn that it was more than worth it. Narbona is out in the middle of the countryside so your own transportation is advisable. narbona.com.uy $$$$$

Where to eat

The hotels above all have good quality restaurants. But if you're looking for something totally alternative...

Lo Korrea, Colonia Estrella

When my friends in Colonia heard I was going to Carmelo, they all insisted I visit on a weekend just to experience Lo Korrea. The enormous country cantina in the Italo-Uruguay Association on the road between the Almacén and El Legado is part of local folklore. Every weekend locals make a pilgrimage to feast upon a fixed menu of home-made *matambre*—stuffed, rolled and boiled beef—with potato salad, followed by home-made all-you-can-eat ravioli and a piece of chicken, unlimited servings of sixteen(!) home-made desserts, tea and coffee and soft drinks and house wine. All for 470 pesos. Open Saturday evening and Sunday lunch with live music

Chivito stand, downtown Carmelo

Just off the main highstreet (Uruguay) on the corner of Lavalleja street, Guillermo Ferreyra's food truck sells home-made hamburgers made from hand-minced 100% beef, (river) fish *milanesas* and home-made fries carefully prepared from scratch. Order, go for a stroll along the riverbank, return, uncork the bottle of wine you bought earlier (no corkage) and tuck in. Open daily lunch and dinner, closed Sundays

Getting around

Biking Plan to get around the vineyards by bike. If you are staying in Colonia Estrella, you are a very short bike ride to most vineyards. Biking from the centre of Carmelo to Colonia Estrella takes 20-30 minutes along quiet roads.

Taxis Your hotel or vineyard will be happy to call you a cab. A cab from the town centre to Colonia Estrella takes under ten minutes and costs about 300 pesos. Hotels out of town will pick you up at the station or port free of charge.

Buses I don't recommend using buses. They are very infrequent and drop you off on the highway leaving you with 2-3 kilometres walk to the vineyards.

When to visit Carmelo

Best seasons Spring and autumn can be the best times to visit for optimum temperatures. The leaves turn colour in May. Carmelo is very hot in the summer time with significant insect presence. See *Practical Tips, Holidays & festivals* for festivals

Go midweek Argentinians and Brazilians have gotten in on the Uruguayan Tuscan secret earlier than the rest of the world and as neighbours they tend to visit on weekends. Savour the experience of a being the sole visitors in a vineyard by going midweek. Some hotels also have cheaper midweek rates.

How long to stay If you have the time spend at least three days and two nights and visit just one or two vineyards a day. Cycle lazily out to each winery, savouring the hours-long wine-tasting sessions. Splash around in the river or in your hotel pool. And have a picnic under a shady tree in the dusky afternoon.

How to get to Carmelo

R21 km 253 Montevideo (3 h) Colonia (1 h) Flores (2 h 30 m) Paysandú (4 h)

Driving From Montevideo, take the R1 to the outskirts of Colonia del Sacramento and turn right onto the R21. From Flores take the R3 to Trinidad, the R57 to Conchillas and then the R21. From Paysandú take the R24 (unpaved) to Fray Bentos (See *Estancias, La Paz, Things to do*), R2 to Mercedes and R21 to Carmelo.

Bus From Montevideo buses (Intertur, Sabelin, Chadre) leave every few hours (3 h 15 m). From Colonia del Sacramento buses (Berrutti) leave every 1-2 hours (1 h 30 m) with less frequency on weekends. From Paysandú there are just two buses per day.

Direct ferry from Buenos Aires You can sail direct to Carmelo on a lesser-known ferry (Cacciola) which sails from a suburb of Buenos Aires through the Tigre delta and up the River Plate twice a day (2h 30m). You can travel independently to Tigre by train or buy a ticket which includes a bus from the centre of Buenos Aires. The total journey from the centre of Buenos Aires to Carmelo takes 5 hours. You can buy tickets online from the ferry site which is in Spanish only.

East coast – Maldonado & Atlantida

Inland from the Atlantic Ocean less than a one-hour drive from Punta del Este and José Ignacio lies Uruguay's most exciting wine-growing region. These picturesque sierras—low-lying hills—have rocky soils of gravel, limestone and weathered granite with some quartz and schist which are hopeless for growing most crops and ideal for growing grapes. This is Uruguay's coolest region with a broad range of temperatures and cool nights, helpful when grapes are ripening. The rocky slopes drain well which is needed as there's a fair amount of rain.

A massive billion-dollar vineyard Bodega Garzón owned by an Argentine oil and gas magnate has set up on 10,000 acres in this area, reportedly impressed by the wines from pioneer vineyard Alto de la Ballena. We're not going to cover Garzón—they really don't need any help from us—but this is such an enormous enterprise that it will undoubtedly change the face of Uruguayan wine-making and Uruguay's name internationally.

We've also grouped Viñedo de los Vientos here which is in Atlantida in the department of Canelones and shares a similar climate.

Alto de la Ballena

Alto de la Ballena—or Whale Heights—is a small vineyard a short drive from Punta del Este, set on a rocky hillside with a panoramic view of a distant lagoon. It was founded by a couple from Montevideo who despite getting into the wine business later in life have pioneered wine-making in these mineral-rich hills and are producing some of the best wines in Uruguay, introducing unique blends onto the national scene in the process. Join them for a highly professional, yet highly personal visit where the wine-tasting takes place on a deck surrounded by pampas grass and overlooking the ocean.

Alvaro Lorenzo and Paula Pivel weren't even wine-drinkers until their late twenties. They were invited to a wine-tasting at the South African Embassy, their taste-buds were peaked and they joined a wine club. Not long after they started holidaying in wine-producing destinations. A few years later looking to buy land, they wanted the investment to pay for itself and decided to start a vineyard and focus on high-end wines and wine tourism. They took almost a year to choose the land which today has just over eight hectares (20 acres) planted with five varieties. They produce 50,000 bottles a year and eight labels. In Europe a winery of this size would produce just one or two wines, says Paula.

The most popular wine sold at Alto de la Ballena is their Tannat-Viognier blend (15% Viognier). The pairing came through a happy coincidence. The couple had planned to produce a Syrah-Viognier blend inspired by the Côte-Rôtie region in France. However the half hectare of Syrah planted didn't produce a harvest that year so they decided to experiment with Viognier. They produced very few bottles but people loved it. Since then this full-bodied Tannat appealing to all palates has been the Alto calling card. Paula confesses in the price range her favourite wine is actually their Merlot. She explains that Uruguay has the perfect *terroir*—a French term for the combination of soil and climate—for Merlot and that those produced in Uruguay can be are outstanding.

Wine-tastings

Tastings take place on a hilltop deck. There's a classic tasting from 32 USD (4 wines) and a premium tasting at 50 USD (6 wines). The wine-tasting is accompanied by cheeses and breads. Morning visits are scheduled at 11.30am. The afternoon visit is scheduled to coincide with sunset. Your visit is likely to stretch out to two hours or more as you relax take in the views and enjoy the breeze. Paula speaks excellent English. Visits by appointment only. Email her at paula.pivel@altodelaballena.com

How to get to Alto de la Ballena

R12 km 16.4 The vineyard is very easily located on the panoramic R12 coming from Punta Ballena.

Viñedo de los Vientos, Atlantida

Pablo Fallabrino is a surfer and radical wine-maker. Descended from an illustrious line of wine-makers—his grandfather, an Italian immigrant from Piedmont, owned the largest winery in Uruguay in the 1950s and 60s—he took over a family vineyard in 1995. Uruguay's *terroir* is very apt for Italian varietals and Pablo imported Nebbiola, Moscato, Arneis—several varieties that his grandfather originally planted here.

The seventeen hectares (around forty acres) of chalky clay soil—excellent for producing complex wines—is just over two miles from the sea and constantly blown by cool winds from the South Atlantic. Pablo called the vineyard Winery of the Winds in honour of the wind's power. He says that as a surfer he's always aware of the wind.

Nationally Pablo is known for breaking the rules of wine-making with remarkable results but he sees it more simply. He says his lack of technical background has been his greatest asset. He likes to produce wine that he is interested in drinking himself, and he wants those wines to be untouched and pure as possible.

Vientos wines are as close to organic as possible, with tiny doses of herbicides and no insecticides. Constant sea breezes keep the vines in maximum health. I saw pagoda trellising in use for the only time on my travels around Uruguayan vineyards, the wind whipping above and below the trellises.

Their new Anarkía Tannat is the "maximum expression of non-intervention," says Pablo. The dramatic label shows his own closed fist crushing a bunch of grapes. I'm not sure how much I like the label but it seems my compatriots do. After samples were sent over to the UK, a first export agreement was quickly hammered out and it can be found on the wine-list at The Fat Duck, one of the UK's five Michelin three-star restaurants. It's also the only wine to make it onto our two Guru'Guay wine lists.

Viñedo de los Vientos exports almost a hundred percent of their wines with a few select stockists in Montevideo.

Wine-tastings

Standard wine-tasting includes four wines accompanied by cheeses and breads. 35 USD. Consult for lunch and tasting options. A three-course lunch with wines costs 96 USD. Email Pablo and Mariana at info@vinedodelosvientos.com

How to get to Viñedo de los Vientos

Ruta 11 km 162. Take the IB to Atlantida and then head north to Estación Atlantida 4 km. The wineyard is on the left and well signposted. Open daily by appointment only.

Twenty best Uruguayan wines

Liber Pisciottano and Nicolas Cappellini only stock local wines at their excellent wine-bar Montevideo Wine Experience, and Liber represents Uruguay in wine-tasting events, so they seemed like the ideal people to put together a selection of Uruguay's best twenty wines[31]. Not only did they take up the challenge, but they ranked their choices. Brave men.

1. Los Nadies *Ímpetu 2011* Manuel Filgueira made just 300 bottles of this exceptional wine. Aged in oak for three years, give it your undivided attention and savour a work of art.

2. Los Cerros de San Juan *Mil Botellas Pentavarietal 2013* Produced by Uruguay's oldest winery, this is one of Uruguay's best reds with an unrivalled quality-price ratio. Aged in oak for two years and then in the bottle for a further twelve months.

3. Los Nadies *Equilibrio Tannat Merlot 2011* Only a totally obsessive wine-maker—capable of binning an entire harvest if it's not up to his expectations—makes wines of this calibre and purity of expression.

4. Estancia La Cruz *Jano Tannat* This wine made by Estela de Frutos, one of Uruguay's foremost wine-makers, is tantamount to sampling a piece of Uruguayan wine-making history. Made from grapes grown on vines that are more than 85 years old, it has subtle tannins and delicate aromas and is a unique experience.

5. Cerro Chapeu *1752 Petit Manseng-Sauvignon Gris* Simply the best white wine in Uruguay. It's elegant and unforgettable. You'll want to keep this to drink in the future.

6. Carrau *Amat Tannat 2011* One of Uruguay's most emblematic Tannats with berry, leather and oak aromas. Beautifully balanced and elegant and will age superbly.

7. Alto de la Ballena *Cetus Cuvée 2011* The purest expression of the Maldonado *terroir*. A delicate, profound and complex blend of Cabernet Franc, Merlot and Syrah.

---

31 Vintage is only included when climatic conditions were decisive in the production of a really exceptional version of a particular wine.

8. Los Nadies *Gwürztraminer-Chardonnay 2009* A rare species—a very complex white. Don't miss the the magnificent aromas of linden flower (*tilo* in Spanish) and honey.

9. Antigua Bodega Stagnari *Osiris Merlot 2007* Uruguay produces really excellent Merlot. This delicate version has a heady bouquet of cassis and chocolate.

10. Giménez Méndez *Tannat Premium* What a typical Tannat should taste like. Packs a punch on the palate, with very clean tannins.

11. Garzón *Albariño Reserva* A giant expression of this white thanks to the mineral-packed soils of Maldonado.

12. Alto de la Ballena *Tannat-Viognier* A French-style blend aged in the barrel for nine months. Experience the potency of the Tannat and the subtle aromas of the Viognier.

13. Pizzorno *Select Blend* A complex Tannat-based blend with a nose of ripe blackberries and a certain elegance thanks to its time in the barrel.

14. Pizzorno *Don Prospero Sauvignon Blanc* Perhaps the best example of a Uruguayan Sauvignon. Very fresh with a citrus nose.

15. Viña Edén *Chardonnay* Incredible minerality and complexity. Perhaps somewhat overpriced but a fine example of a Uruguayan white wine.

16. Pisano *RPF Tannat* Perfect for lovers of big personality wines. Enjoy with beef.

17. Viñedo de los Vientos *Anarkía Tannat* A winery that's always breaking the play-book. Here Pablo Fallabrino cuts out pesticides and sulfites, to produce an almost organic version of the Uruguay classic. Ideal with roast beef, lamb or game.

18. Artesana *Tannat Rosé* Wonderfully versatile. Pair with fish, beef and pasta.

19. Los Cerros de San Juan *Cuna de Piedra Tannat* A great Tannat for under ten dollars. Fresh fruit aromas, very balanced tannins and hints of barrel ageing.

20. Giménez Méndez *Alta Reserva Arinarnoa* Another lower-priced red, well-balanced and fresh with a nice structure and notes of menthol and blueberries.

Best wines for around ten dollars or less

Viviana del Rio and Claudio Angelotti run Bodegas del Uruguay, the only website exclusively dedicated to Uruguayan wines. They give Guru'Guay their top picks for people who like wine but don't want to pay an arm and a leg for the privilege.

Pizzorno *Don Próspero Tannat Maceración Carbónica* 230 pesos A great Tannat starter wine. Because of the way its been made, you can appreciate the aromas and flavour of Tannat without the tannins. Great with pastas and meats of all kinds.

Viñedo de los Vientos *Anarkía Tannat* 295 pesos It's back!

Irurtia *Km.0 Río de la Plata Gran Reserva Pinot Noir* 270 pesos Garnet-coloured and harmonious, expressing the best of Carmelo. Pair with complete opposites—very spicy or barely seasoned dishes.

H. Stagnari *Tannat Premier* 235 pesos A young red produced in Salto, one of the most interesting *terroirs* in Uruguay. Great with stews (*guisos*) and strong cheeses.

Giménez Méndez *Alta Reserva Sauvignon Blanc* 250 pesos A classic that's excellent year after year. A very refreshing, pale white with intense aromas. Drink as an aperitif.

Familia Deicas *Don Pascual Reserve Viognier* 220 pesos Uruguayans are really going for this smooth white with its bright amber colour, fruity aromas and long finish. Great with chicken and seafood.

Marichal *Premium Varietal Chardonnay* 175 pesos An excellent well-balanced white. Pair with fish, seafood, sweetbreads (*mollejas*) and vegetarian dishes.

Garzón Estate *Cabernet de Corte* 305 pesos A bright ruby red blend. Fresh and silky. Cabernet Franc dominates along with Tannat, Merlot and Marselan.

Viña Varela Zarranz *María Zarranz Extra Brut* 370 pesos OK, this goes over budget but as it's sparkling then perhaps you're celebrating. This brilliant white was made by traditional methods. Drink it on its own or to accompany a meal from the start to the very finish.

Private wine tours

Uruguay has a very strict drink driving law—you cannot have even a single glass and drive. So a private wine tour is a great way to experience some of these great little vineyards.

Borravino Tours – Carmelo and Montevideo

Damian Piñón was born in Mendoza in the heart of Argentine wine country and is currently based in Colonia. He offers private wine tours to Carmelo, Montevideo and Canelones. He also designs and leads tours in Argentina. Damian's other passion is history, especially of Uruguay and South America. If you're thinking of making a wine safari around Uruguay and Argentina this born-and-bred South American wine enthusiast could well be your man. His expertise, attention to detail and engaging manner, coupled with his wealth of historical knowledge gives you the opportunity to comprehend the complexities of this most fascinating part of the world. From major wineries in the foothills of the Andes in Mendoza to the fourth-generation family-owned vineyards in Uruguay, Damian offers a plethora of venues each showcasing something unique. When Damian is not leading other wine enthusiasts around South America he is at home in Colonia making his own artisanal wine.

Contact Damian at Borravino Wine Tours damian@borravinowinetours.com for a 10% discount using the code GURU1.

Tour prices from 145 USD per person

Practical Tips
Getting to Uruguay

Uruguay is on the east of the South American continent, wedged between two giants, Argentina and Brazil. Uruguayans affectionately call their country "*el paisito*"—the little country—though in reality it is actually slightly bigger than the state of Florida (USA).

Most people coming from Buenos Aires take the ferry. From Brazil most fly.

Airports

The vast majority of flights come into the **Carrasco International Airport (MVD)** twelve miles (20 km) east of Montevideo.

The **Aeropuerto Internacional Capitan Corbeta Curbelo (PDP)**, the tiny yet chic international airport in Punta del Este receives just two daily direct flights, one from Buenos Aires and the other from São Paulo. During high season the number of flights increases to 5-6 per day including possibly from Chile and Rio de Janeiro[32]. The airport is very close to Punta Ballena and thirty minutes from the centre of Punta.

---

32 Regional airline routes are confirmed very late in the year. Checking in September, all airlines were still to confirm their summer routes. Sky (from Chile) and Amaszonas (Paraguay) were among the indecisive. We recommend you check online.

Driving

Rental companies will not allow you to cross international borders.

From Buenos Aires (Argentina)

Montevideo There are two direct ferries (Buquebus) a day (2 h 15 m). Most people use the cheaper ferry-and-bus services (Buquebus, Seacat and Colonia Express) which involves ferry to Colonia (1 h) and then bus on to Montevideo (2 h 15 m). Including transfer time the total journey takes 4-5 hours. Three overnight bus services (CAUVI, El Condor and Belgrano) run daily from Buenos Aires to Montevideo (8 h).

You can fly in 40 minutes but the Guru recommends taking the ferry[33]. If you decide to fly, be aware that Buenos Aires has two airports—the international airport known as Ezeiza (EZE) which is outside of the capital and the national airport Aeroparque (AEP) in the city centre itself. Save yourself time and money by getting your flight from Aeroparque unless you are already at Ezeiza.

Colonia del Sacramento Several ferries (Buquebus, Seacat and Colonia Express) each day (50 m).

Carmelo (wine country!) A picturesque ferry travels twice a day from the Tigre delta to the town of Carmelo. The total journey from the centre of Buenos Aires takes about 5 hours.

Punta del Este Aerolineas Argentinas runs one daily direct flight to and from Buenos Aires (AEP) year round. During high season (December-March) depending on demand a second flight may be added.

---

33 www.guruguay.com/what-is-the-best-way-to-travel-from-buenos-aires-to-montevideo

From the Argentina interior

Overnight buses (EGA, Encon, Copay and Nossar) run several times a week from Mendoza, Cordoba and Rosario to different destinations in Uruguay including Montevideo, Paysandú, Tacuarembó and elsewhere. International buses have very comfortable sleeper beds.

Flying During high season a route from Rosario to Punta del Este may become available.

From Brazil

Flying You are likely to want to fly from São Paulo (2 h 45 m) and Rio de Janeiro (3 h). From southern Brazil (Porto Alegre) there is a one-hour flight.

Direct flights are available from São Paulo, Porto Alegre and Rio de Janeiro to Montevideo. Choose from LATAM, GOL and Azul. There is one daily São Paulo-Punta del Este flight with LATAM.

Bus Porto Alegre is the biggest Brazilian city closest to Uruguay. Buses (EGA and TTL) travel from Porto Alegre to Montevideo in ten hours stopping along the coast at Punta del Este, San Carlos, Chuy and elsewhere. There are also buses from the Brazilian resort Florianopolis. They also travel to other cities in Uruguay including Tacuarembó and Paysandú. The price difference between flying and the bus is negligible.

From Chile

The excellent LATAM and a low cost airline Sky fly to Montevideo.

From the Iguazú Falls

Unfortunately there are currently no direct flights. Flights to Iguazú go via Buenos Aires (Aerolineas Argentinas) and São Paulo (LATAM). With optimal connections it's likely to take you at least six hours to fly from Iguazú to Montevideo. I recommend staying overnight in Buenos Aires to break up the trip.

Flying from other Latin American countries

There are direct flights to Montevideo from Chile, Panama, Peru, Paraguay and Bolivia. Fly from Panama with COPA, Lima (Peru) with Avianca, Santa Cruz (Bolivia) and Asunción (Paraguay) with Amaszonas. Most land in the early hours of the morning. Amaszonas may fly direct to Punta del Este in high season.

From Europe, North America and the rest of the world

There are few direct flights to Uruguay. You will usually have to go through Buenos Aires or São Paulo. European carriers include Air Europa, Air France and Iberia. American Airlines is the only airline travelling direct to Montevideo from the US however their service is not great. I recommend using good Latin American airlines like LATAM, Avianca and COPA. Guru'Guay readers have saved up to 500 dollars on tickets rather than going with US or European carriers.

More reading on GuruGuay.com

Having trouble comparing ferry ticket prices[34] online? Here's a little matrix I update periodically. Read the Guru analysis of the best and worst airlines flying into Montevideo[35].

---

34 www.guruguay.com/ferry-prices-buenos-aires-uruguay/
35 www.guruguay.com/flying-to-uruguay/

When to visit

Uruguay is a temperate country with four seasons, the opposites of seasons in the northern hemisphere.

Summer (December-February) These are the hottest months with daily averages of around 90°F. Around New Year temperatures can rise above 100°F for a few days. Periodic rain and cloud can hit at any point and may last up to four days.

Fall (March-May) It's possible to swim until April when the waters are warmest after heating up all summer. These months are particularly lovely weather-wise. Days are mild (70°F), and there are frequent Indian summers. Nights are chilly from March.

Winter (June-August) Even during the coldest months, the average sunlight hours are 6-7 hours a day. It's rare to have rain for more than a few days in a row and there are periodic Indian summers. It is always several degrees warmer inland than at the coast during the day. Despite reasonably balmy temperatures (60°F) you may feel much colder than you would expect in the shade because of humidity.

Spring (September-November) With temperatures around 70°F, spring is a wonderful time to visit. September and October may be too cold for swimming though Europeans will undoubtedly be happy to jump in on a sunny day. Days are mild though there can still be cold snaps. It's the prefect time to visit an estancia as the countryside is in full bloom and there are newborn animals.

High season

There are three peaks in high season. Christmas and New Year are the busiest time of the year at the beach. Revellers from Brazil and Argentina and locals flood in with family and friends to celebrate the holidays between **December 24 to January 10**. Uruguayans hit the beaches in full force during **Carnival week** and **Easter week**. Easter is typically considered the last opportunity to take a holiday before the work year starts. (I'm serious. There's an expression here that says "The year doesn't start till the last cyclist of the Easter race has made it over the finishing line".)

Holidays & festivals

Public holidays

Major bank holidays January 1, May 1, July 18, August 25 and December 25
Other bank holidays January 6, April 19, May 18, June 19, October and November 2

You will not really notice public holidays at the beach or in the countryside. It is quite different in Montevideo where on major bank holidays most shops close and transport runs on a minimal schedule[36]. On Christmas Eve and New Year's Eve taxis and buses stop around 4pm and will not start back up till 5-6am. Uruguay has very strong labour laws and May 1, Workers' Day, is possibly the most strictly observed holiday of the year with no public transport at all.

The **carnival** holiday is the Monday and Tuesday before Ash Wednesday. Most Uruguayans take the entire week and head to the beach.

---

36 Find out why by reading *Why does the tourist industry in Montevideo close down at peak visitor times?*
www.guruguay.com/montevideo-closed-peak-season

Festivals & celebrations

Make sure you plan your trip to coincide with a festival or two. The biggest festival in Uruguay is **carnival** which takes place all over the country with the largest and longest celebrations happening in Montevideo[37] for forty nights between late January and early March.

In recent years the **wine** industry has realised that people want to celebrate the cycle of production. Nowadays there are multiple festivals, the classic being the **Tannat and Lamb festival** in May and **harvest** in February and early March. The countryside is at the heart of Uruguayan society. **Gaucho and folk music and dance festivals** take place all year round in the countryside, in Montevideo and in rural towns close to the beach.

We included a selection of some of the best festivals to check out and where to stay.

January

- 'Andresito le canta al pais' Festival, Flores - a music and folklore festival on the banks of the stunning Andresito lake [stay at *Estancias, La Estiria*]
- 'Pueblo de Gregorio Aznarez canta' Festival, Gregorio Aznarez – small folk fair with music, enormous barbecues, old-fashioned stands [stay at *Beaches, Punta Ballena*]
- San Gregorio Festival, Tacuarembó – in a quaint town of painted murals [stay at *Estancias, Yvytu Itaty*]
- Festival de la Doma y el Folclore, Nueva Palmira – folklore festival and rodeo [near *Wine Country, Carmelo*]
- Carnival rehearsals and inaugural carnival parade [stay in Montevideo]
- Colonia Week [stay in Colonia del Sacramento]

February

- Festival del Gaucho (Gaucho Festival), Tala, Canelones [stay at *Beaches, Atlantida*]
- National Wine-grape Festival (Festival Nacional de la Uva), Carmelo [in *Wine Country, Carmelo*]
- Nightly carnival *tablado* shows at different venues and the two-night *Llamadas* Carnival Parade [stay in Montevideo]

---

37 6 reasons why you must not miss carnival in Montevideo www.guruguay.com/montevideo-carnival

March

- Wine Harvest (Festival de la Vendimia) [throughout *Wine Country*]
- Fiesta of the Gaucho Nation (Fiesta de la Patria Gaucha), Tacuarembó – Uruguay's biggest gaucho gathering [stay at *Estancias, Yvytu Itaty*]
- Fiesta de la Doma y el Folclore (Folklore and Rodeo), Lascano [*Beaches, Punta del Diablo*]

April

- Semana Criolla Patria Grande – a week long gaucho bash over Easter [stay in Montevideo]
- Encuentro de Salsipuedes, Guichon, Paysandú – commemoration of a historic deception and massacre of Uruguay's indigenous peoples [stay at *Estancias, La Paz*]
- Criollas del Parque Roosevelt, Costa de Oro – week-long gaucho rodeos and fair in a forest [stay at *Beaches, Atlantida and the Costa de Oro* or in *El Pinar*]

May

- Criolla de las Chincillas, Atlantida – May 1st gaucho festival [stay at *Beaches, Atlantida*]
- Jornada de Jineteadas y Domas, Trinidad – gaucho festival [stay at *Estancias, La Estiria*]
- Horse Festival (Fiesta del Caballo), Rural del Prado, Montevideo [stay in Montevideo]

June

- Festival Tannat y Cordero (Tannat and Lamb Festival) – vineyards offer elaborate four-course lunches with lashings of wine over a weekend [throughout *Wine Country*]
- San Cono, Florida – Uruguay's most famous religious festival [stay at *Estancias, El Ceibo*]
- 23-24 San Juan Bonfires (Noche de San Juan) – bonfires and music [stay in *Montevideo, La Pedrera* and all across *Wine Country*]

July

- La Yerra – neutering and branding of livestock, one of the most important rural celebrations of the year [stay at *Estancias*]

August

- Los Patricios del 25, Florida – three days of gaucho festivities, horse parades and live music to celebrate Uruguay's declaration of independence [stay at *Estancias, El Ceibo*]
- Pruning Month (Mes de la Poda y Cocina criolla) – vineyards open their doors to demonstrate pruning techniques and organise gourmet events focusing on local cuisine [throughout *Wine Country*]

September
- Expo Prado – week-long agricultural fair in its 110+ edition [stay in Montevideo]
- Gaucho Spring Festival (Fiesta de la Primavera Gaucha), 19 de abril [stay *Beaches, La Paloma*]

October
- Wild Boar[38] Festival (Festival de Tradicion, Jabali y Aventura), Aiguá – hunting, music and gauchos for those of strong disposition [stay at *Beaches, Punta del Este*]
- Fiesta del Jabali, Lorenzo Geyres, Paysandú – wild boar hunting and festivities [stay at *Estancias, La Paz*]

November
- San Ramon Festival, Canelones – horse parades and live music [stay *Estancias, El Ceibo*]
- Wine Tourism Day (Día del Enoturismo) – Uruguay joins vineyards the world over to celebrate with three days of events [throughout *Wine Country*]

December
- Festival de Fogones del Cerro de Nico Perez - town party with music and bonfires in Nico Perez, Florida [stay at *Estancias, Los Platanos*]
- Fiesta de la Madera, Piedras Coloradas, Paysandú – country fair where lumberjacks show off their skills with axe and chainsaw [stay at *Estancias, La Paz*]
- Festival del Mate, Rocha – the city of Rocha celebrates Uruguay's favourite drink with music and shows [stay at *Beaches, La Paloma*]
- Procession of the Virgin of Itati, Villa Ansina, Tacuarembó – a Virgin uniting Uruguay's indigenous, Afro and gaucho heritages in a lost town [stay at *Estancias, Yvytu Itaty*]
- Fiesta Gardeliana, Tacuarembó – the unexpectedly rural birthplace of tango's most famous artist, Carlos Gardel, celebrates his legacy [stay at *Estancias, Yvytu Itaty*]

Note We didn't include dates as they change from year to year and are not confirmed until last minute. Yes, welcome to Latin America. We chose festivals close to the beaches and ranches in this guide that last more than one day to maximise your chance of attending. Contact your accommodation and ask for recommendations.

---

38 These hunts are sponsored by the local government to keep numbers of these enormous animals (which are not native to Uruguay) under control.

What to bring

Uruguay is on the high end of so-called developing countries. You'll find everything you need but because Uruguay has a very small market anything imported tends to be pricey. So clothes and electronic items are much more expensive and there's significantly less choice than what you may be used to at home.

Travel adaptors and voltage

The most common plug is international type C[39] and F. Type L is also used and type I especially close to the Argentine border. Don't worry if you forget your adaptor. Large supermarkets and your local Uruguayan hardware store or *ferreteria* (no small furry animal jokes please) will stock them. Ask for an *adaptador de enchufe* (ad-ap-ta-DOR day en-CHOO-fay). They cost 2-4 USD.

The voltage in Uruguay is 220V. Your phone, computer and tablet should all automatically convert.

What to wear

Uruguayans take pride in being a very **egalitarian society**. No one likes to stand out and that includes regarding attitude and dress. It's almost impossible to distinguish a rich local from a regular one by their clothes. Even going out to the dinner or the theatre in the capital, you'll see that invariably **people dress (very) casually**. During the daytime shorts are totally fine in the city though younger women may attract unwanted attention.

At the beach and in the countryside the dress code is so laid-back as to be non-existent. Anyone tottering along the sandy streets of Punta del Diablo in high heels is definitely not a Uruguayan.

---

39 www.iec.ch/worldplugs/typeC.htm

In summer pack light, very light

The temperatures will be in the high nineties and even at the most chic of destinations there's no need for anything fancy. Believe me, that little cocktail dress will never see the light of day. The essentials are a bathing suit, sarong (called a *pareo*), T-shirt, shorts, flip-flops or sandals. Take a light throw or fleece for the evening and a waterproof wind-breaker in case it rains. You'll need a hat, sunglasses (the light here is particularly luminous) and lots of sunscreen.

In fall and spring, add a warm layer

Still pack light but add long trousers and bring an additional warm layer.

In winter, bring easy on–off layers

The sun comes out, you boil. The sun goes behind a cloud and you freeze. These rapid temperature changes make it really easy to catch a cold as soon as you arrive. Be prepared to beat the sniffles by bringing layers that you can take on and off without thinking twice. The essentials are a T-shirt, long-sleeved shirt, fleece, water-proof wind-breaker, warm footwear, gloves and a hat that covers your ears (for early mornings and windy days). If you are going to one of the more rustic estancias or staying at a beach house, take warm pyjamas and slippers.

Riding and at the estancia

Wear long trousers even in summer to avoid being chaffed by the saddle or scratched by thorns on more adventurous rides. No flip-flops or sandals. Closed shoes that are also good for walking are best.

How to look like you've stepped out of an edition of South American Tatler Get

thee to a *talabarteria*—as gaucho stockists are called—and buy *bombachas* (trousers with side pleats and ankle cuffs*)* and soft leather riding boots. Make sure that they are beige or khaki. Even if you don't ride, you'll totally look the part. Uruguayan men wear traditional *alpargatas* (jute-soled slippers with textile uppers) when lounging around on the estancia. You can pick them up in any supermarket for a few dollars and in trendy shoe stores for significantly more.

Driving and car hire

Outside of the capital, Uruguay is a very easy country to get around by car. National highways are largely empty two-lane roads and you can get around easily using an old-fashioned paper map.

Driving regulations

Speed limits 120 km per hour on the IB, 110 km on other major highways and 90 km on smaller highways. In towns the speed limit is 45 km but this can vary, for instance there are parts of Montevideo where you can drive up to 75 km. Always look out for speed signs.

Turn on your low-beam headlights at all times It's obligatory anywhere in Uruguay.

Safety belts are obligatory. As are crash helmets and reflective jackets for cyclists and motor bikers.

Drink driving There is zero alcohol tolerance for drivers. Drivers even minutely over the limit will have their licence confiscated. US nationals get their licence back in the US and will be slapped with the corresponding penalties for DUI. Brits will have their licences sent to the DVLA. Other licences are sent to the corresponding consulate in Montevideo. This law has effected the wine industry no end. Watch Guru'Guay[40] for updates on the situation.

No bribes Perhaps contrary to your experience in other countries, do not try to bribe the Uruguayan police. This will get you into serious trouble.

Highways

Uruguay's highways between major tourist destinations i.e. Colonia to Montevideo to Punta del Este to Punta del Diablo are in great shape.

The largest highway is the Interbalnearia or IB—the coastal highway between the

---

40 www.guruguay.com/drink-drive-uruguay

airport in Montevideo and Punta del Este. The IB has two lanes each way. Most highways in the interior are two-lane roads with no central reservation. Yes, they are small but it's no problem because there's very little traffic. The highways are called *rutas* and we refer to them that way here. So Highway 10 is Ruta 10 or R10.

Road-markers and locations There are road-markers along all highways set one kilometre apart. The road-marker tells you the number of kilometres you are from a major intersection. Addresses in the countryside or at the beach are typically given this way: Ruta 7 km 145.5. This means, on the Ruta 7 highway turn 500 metres after the marker for km 145. Uruguayans count blocks as 100 metres, so an address is given as km 50.200 means that your exit is the second road after the km 50 marker.

Leaving the airport The Carrasco International Airport is almost at the start of the IB at what would be the 20 km marker. Heading to the beach, drive out of the airport, turn left at the roundabout and the first right immediately is to the IB. To Montevideo take a right at the roundabout.

Tolls There are number of tolls along Uruguayan highways. The standard charge in 2017 was 85 pesos payable in Uruguayan pesos and dollars as well as currencies from Argentina and Brazil. So civilised. Tolls are charged both ways.

Driving tips in the interior

Driving in Uruguay is a real pleasure in part because outside of the larger towns there are so few cars on the road. However the state of many inland highways can add an unexpected frisson of adventure tourism to your travel. I don't mean you need a 4x4 to get around, but you do need to take your time.

Take GoogleMap travel times as a very approximate guide as Google does not take into account the condition of highways in the interior. At times you will have to slow down to 60 km per hour or less because of poor or unpaved road surfaces. I have added conservative times in consultation with locals, however always consult your local hosts for travel advice.

Respect road signs especially regarding overtaking (double yellow lines in the centre of the road). Road surfaces may not be great, but signage is usually very good.

Beware of cows It's common to run into livestock being herded across a highway.

Sundown The gently rolling countryside provides little shade when driving west in the late afternoon and the sun will obscure your vision. Reach your destination well before sundown.

Greet fellow travellers Drivers and bystanders typically raise a hand to greet each other. Greet gauchos on horseback, road workers filling in pot holes and other folk you pass. They will undoubtedly be the same folks that will help you out if you have the bad luck to get a flat tyre.

Calculate more time than you would normally take for your journey and sit back and relax on some of the emptiest roads in the world.

Driving in Montevideo

I don't recommend having a car when you stay in Montevideo. It's a comparatively small city which is very walkable depending on the neighbourhood. In the Old City you can walk absolutely everywhere you need to go. There's also a very good public transportation network of buses, taxis and services like Uber and Cabify. And truth be told, get a normally lovely Montevidean granny behind the wheel and she becomes the devil in disguise. Hire a car the day you plan to leave Montevideo and the rest of the time enjoy making real contact with the city on foot and being driven by locals.

What you should know about car hire in Uruguay

International car rental companies are all present along with a number of local companies.

Deductible It is standard practice to sign a credit card voucher for a *deductible* to the tune of 1000 USD for a compact car and more for a larger car. This means that insurance covers you for everything except the first thousand dollars worth of damage. The voucher will be ripped up at the end of your rental.

VAT-off car rental[41] To encourage tourism, the Uruguayan government has discounted the VAT on car hire for the last few years. Chances are this generous benefit will continue indefinitely. The offer applies to all non-Uruguayan credit and debit cards.

Recommended car hire company

I get asked all the time about reliable car hire in Uruguay. I have been recommending a local company Mariño Sport with offices in Montevideo, Colonia and Punta del Este to our guesthouse clients and my own friends and family since 2010 and have been consistently impressed by their great service and personal touch. My guest Pooja from Chicago left her car lights on overnight and the battery went flat. She called the Mariño emergency number and the mechanic was there to help her in no time for no charge. Just one of many stories that I could tell.

Drop-off and pick-up wherever you request This is a great part of the service. Mariño will meet you at the airport, the port or your hotel and then they will pick the car up from you wherever you decide for free in Montevideo. You can drop-off and pick-up in Colonia and Punta del Este for a small additional fee.

Reliable cars Mariño is the official service representative for Nissan, Hyundai and Renault and their cars are well-maintained. This may seem a basic requirement, but I have heard enough stories of rental cars breaking down to know that this is not a given.

Automatics and custom motorbikes In Uruguay most cars are stick shift. Mariño has the largest fleet of small and medium-sized automatic cars in Uruguay. They rent custom bikes by Kawasaki.

10% off with Guru'Guay Email car-rental@guruguay.com writing 'Guru'Guay car rental: your name' in the subject line. A word of warning: Don't be put off by their terrible written English, you will work things out.

---

41 www.guruguay.com/use-credit-card-get-vat-off

Public transport

Long-distance buses go all over Uruguay and internationally from the central Tres Cruces bus station in Montevideo. Buses are generally very comfortable with reclining seats and Wi-Fi. Services are frequent and, unless you are buying at very short notice on days of highest demand, you won't have a problem getting tickets.

All information on services in and out of the capital including times, prices and distances are centralised online at the Tres Cruces website[42]. Turn on your online translator and consult the Guru'Guay explainer on how to use the site[43]. It's possible to buy tickets online. Alternatively try giving the companies a call (numbers on the website). I talked to a very helpful English-speaking agent and was able to buy a ticket over the phone giving credit card and passport details.

Getting information before you arrive regarding travelling by bus around the interior is more complicated. There's no one website collecting this information. Your accommodation will be able to give you the most up-to-date advice regarding companies and frequencies.

---

42 www.trescruces.com.uy
43 www.guruguay.com/travelling-by-bus-in-uruguay

Buses between the beaches of Maldonado and Rocha It's usually necessary when travelling by bus between the two departments to change buses at a central terminal. San Carlos (20 mins from Punta del Este) has good connections to most beaches in Maldonado and Rocha. The town of Rocha is also a hub. Neither town has much to interest travellers. La Paloma also has reasonable connections and is a lovely beach town.

Local buses within Montevideo are cheap and frequent. Services within towns in the the rest of Uruguay are generally more limited. The local government maintains this easily consultable online travel map[44] which helps you to plan your journeys by bus or on foot and get around Montevideo like a local.

Taxis are reasonably cheap and reliable all over Uruguay other than in the department of Maldonado. A reasonable price for ten-mile trip is about 350 pesos. In Punta del Este the cabs are amazing, sleek Mercedes and eye-wateringly expensive.

Remises are private cars used for longer trips. Remise companies have offices in bus terminals.

Ride apps are strongly regulated in Uruguay. At the time of writing Uber, Cabify and Easy Taxi can be used in Montevideo and Canelones, and Easy Taxi within Punta del Este. Download the app and punch in the locations you want to travel to, to see if the app works in the area you plan to stay.

---

44 www.guruguay.com/getting-around-montevideo-interactive-map

Food & drink

Mealtimes in Uruguay

Restaurants generally offer lunch from noon with kitchens closing around 3.30pm. Dinner service starts at 8pm and ends around midnight or when the last customer leaves. Uruguayans have lunch at 1pm and dinner at 10pm. A restaurant which stays open all day generally switches to a reduced menu or *cafeteria*—hot drinks, sandwiches and cakes—between 4 and 8pm.

What eating out costs

A cup of coffee 60-120 pesos

A glass of wine 120-150 pesos

A pint of craft beer 120-200 pesos

Main course 280-450 pesos

Dessert 150 pesos

These prices were taken from two good eateries in the capital in 2017. Prices at trendier beach resorts will be (substantially) higher. Prices in the interior tend to be lower. Note that cheap restaurants are not significantly cheaper.

10 foods & beverages to try at the beach and on the estancia

Uruguayans like plain food. Give them a slab of beef and a mixed salad—lettuce and tomato, and maybe onion if they're really pushing the boat out—and they're happy. You too can be content because Uruguayan beef is superb. And look out for these favourites.

Miniaturas Ask for: mee-nee-ah-TOO-raz Bite-size pieces of white fish, dipped in batter or covered in breadcrumbs and deep-fried. Served as an appetizer to share.

Buñuelos de algas Ask for: boo-nweloz day AL-gas A Rocha classic, seaweed fritters are served everywhere from humble fish-stands to the most exclusive restaurants. Seaweed is collected in the morning, added to batter and deep-fried.

Croquetas de sirí Ask for: crow-KEH-taz day see-REE Another Rocha classic, deep-fried croquettes made with sirí crab caught on the coast.

Milanesa de pescado Ask for: mee-la-NAY-sa day peh-SKAH–doh A breaded, deep-fried fish fillet. Most common milanesas are made with beef (*carne*) or chicken (*pollo*). Vegetarian versions include eggplant (*berenjena*). But at the beach, it's gotta be fish. A sandwich version is a *milanesa al pan*.

Galleta de campaña Ask for: guy-ZHET-ah day cam-PAN-yah A square concertina-like biscuit appreciated in the countryside for its long-life. Delicious fresh, it tastes like cardboard after a few days, but revives gloriously when toasted and buttered.

Asado Ask for: aa-SAA-do This favourite cut of ribs is solely flavoured with salt and best savoured in the open air accompanied by salad, bread and a good Tannat.

Guiso Ask for: GEE-so Stews are the stars of the country kitchen. Flavour depends on the region, ingredients in season and grandma's recipe. Try an *ensopado* (vegetables, meat and noodles in broth) or *guiso de arroz*, a rice stew of lamb and vegetables.

Mate Ask for: MA-tay That beverage that every single Uruguayan adult is drinking on the bus, at the beach, in the bank and on the street. A type of tea made with mate leaves, sipped from a gourd through a metal straw. Drinkers add almost boiling water to the gourd from a Thermos flask, a permanent appendage. Argentines, Southern Brazilians and Paraguayans also drink mate but Uruguayans are the only ones to drink mate anytime, any place, anywhere.

Butiá Ask for: boo-tee-YA A bright orange fruit with a sweet and sour flavour which grows on the palm trees in Rocha. Locals use it to make a liqueur (*licor de butiá*) and you'll find *butiá* in everything from ice-cream to elegant sauces to firewater (*caña*).

Personal safety

Uruguay is a very safe country, especially by Latin American standards[45]. But you'd never know this if you talk to Uruguayans who have never travelled. They'll complain that the country, particularly Montevideo, is "dangerous" and wax nostalgic about a time when everyone left their front doors open. My perspective as someone who has lived in the capital for almost twenty years and in lots of other countries as well is that Uruguay a very safe destination. Uruguayans are extremely friendly people and all travellers including solo women can feel comfortable.

In the capital

Montevideo is one of the safest cities in Latin America but it is still a capital city and an unlucky traveller could encounter small-scale crime. Let me give you an illustration. Of all our guesthouse guests last year just one couple experienced crime—a bag snatch—which took place at midday in a residential neighbourhood. They were unlucky. Take the regular precautions that you would when you are in a capital city and you should be just fine. That advice goes for any neighbourhood, the upscale ones too. One thing I would recommend in Montevideo is not to leave anything of value on view in a unattended car. Even a jacket could tempt a break-in.

---

45   In 2017 it was the third safest country after Chile and Costa Rica according to the Global Peace Index.

In the countryside

As I travelled around researching this book I found myself in towns where noone locked their cars and my host left his jacket and helmet on top of his motorbike while we went into a restaurant to eat. In wine country the door of our cabin stayed unlocked the entire three days we were there. Of course be alert and take sensible precautions but you will marvel at how safe it is to travel around.

At the beach

The scene at the beach is very safe—regardless of whether the beach is crowded or empty for miles. As a woman I have never felt worried about taking hours-long solo walks along deserted beaches.

You can feel comfortable about asking a neighbour on the beach to keep an eye on your stuff when you go for a walk or a swim. Say: *"Me lo puedes mirar?"* (meh lo PWAY-des mee-RAH-r) and gesture to your stuff.

There is one crime issue at the beach in Uruguay primarily around New Year and that is the robbery of holiday homes and rentals. There's no danger. The thieves are looking for money and electronic goods and they want to be in and out before you are even aware of them. Houses where the residents are distracted, asleep or out are most targetted. So close and lock windows and doors when you are not in the house or at night. If your accommodation has a safe or alarm use it. If there's no safe, lock larger valuables in your car out of sight. If you don't have a car, I know people that take their valuables with them to the beach (unheard of in Brazil where you are advised to take nothing with you but your wrap). I don't want to make you nervous, just aware if you rent during high season. Off season it would be very bad luck to be burgled.

Staying healthy

You can drink the water

More than 99 percent of the tap water in Uruguay is potable, compared to Europe's average of 93 percent (2015). So yes, you can drink the water.

No need for special vaccinations

Uruguay has such a good health system that lots of retirees from the US are settling here. And the temperate climate means that naturally there are no tropical diseases. So how I chuckled when I saw that the CDC recommends "most travellers" have typhoid shots. I had never heard of typhoid ever in Uruguay. I checked with UN agencies here and apparently there was a completely isolated typhoid outbreak in a geriatric home in 2011. I guess that's what prompted the CDC advice. The same site also recommends not consuming monkeys while in Uruguay. Just as well there are no monkeys. Just make sure your routine vaccinations including tetanus are up to date.

Where to get hospital treatment

If you have the bad luck of falling seriously ill the best treatment centres are in Montevideo.

Smoking tobacco and marijuana

Uruguay was the fourth country in the world to ban smoking in enclosed public places. So you can't smoke inside a café or restaurant but you can smoke at an outdoor table. Take your cue from the locals and only light up if they do. The Uruguayan government became the first in the world to pass legislation to control the entire supply of marijuana with landmark legislation in 2013. Bureaucracy finally saw marijuana go on sale in 2017. Most users grow their own. As a non-resident you cannot buy cannabis but it is totally legal to smoke gifted marijuana[46].

Sunbathing precautions

There is a major hole in the ozone layer over the South Pole and the sun here is more ferocious than in other parts of the world. Between November and March, follow these tips that you'll see the locals adhering to.

- Always wear sunscreen when you are outside during summer even on cloudy days. Apply carefully including to spots you may forget like the back of your neck. Reapply several times during the day.
- Wear sunglasses and a hat.
- Stay out of the sun between noon and 4pm. Go to the beach early, leave at midday, go have lunch, a siesta, and come back no earlier than 4pm (it's light till after 8pm).
- Perhaps invest in a beach umbrella for around 20 USD at most supermarkets.

Lifeguards and warning flags

The most popular beaches in Uruguay have lifeguards during high season. Flag systems may vary from department to department but generally the code is:

- red or red with the word *Peligro* (danger) - don't go in the water
- yellow - bathe with caution
- green - good bathing conditions
- red with a green cross - unsanitary bathing conditions (for example, algae)
- black - storm approaching (occasionally appropriated if lifeguards are on strike).

---

46 Find out more about marijuana in Uruguay www.guruguay.com/foreigners-marijuana-uruguay

Money

Credit and debit cards The most widely accepted credit card in Uruguay by far is VISA with 70% of the market. Mastercard is your best second option. Few places accept American Express and Diners. We recommend travelling with two types of credit card (i.e. Visa and Mastercard) and carrying a few hundred dollars in cash.

Always carry some cash, particularly at the beach Many restaurants and smaller hotels do not accept credit cards[47]. At the beach there may be no static ATM. During the summer months, mobile ATMs frequently run out of cash.

Bring US dollars Euros are also fine, but dollars are more readily exchanged and get better rates. You can exchange your excess pesos back into US dollars losing very little as dollar buying and selling rates are virtually the same. Exchange other currencies in Montevideo before heading to the beach or countryside.

Wait to get Uruguayan pesos when you arrive All my guests who have tried getting hold of pesos before they travel have gotten very bad rates—if they have been able to get hold of pesos at all. The airport, port or bus station in Montevideo have ATMs. Avoid the airport exchange which has notoriously poor rates.

Where to exchange money Most Uruguayans will use a *cambio* or money exchange rather than a bank. *Cambios* are open regular business hours, typically 9 am till 7 pm Monday to Friday and Saturdays 9am-1pm, whereas banks open Monday to Friday from 1pm to 5pm.

No commission charged for exchanging money Rates are displayed in the store windows and varies little from one *cambio* to the next. There's no need to take ID with you when exchanging, and no commission is charged. It's all super easy.

Withdraw dollars not pesos ATMs in Uruguay dispense both dollars and pesos. There are two ATM networks—Red BROU and Banred. Uruguayan banks have imposed a 5000-peso withdrawal limit on foreign cards. Banred has a 300 USD limit per

---

47 Greedy credit card companies charge a 6% commission—a percentage that smaller businesses can ill-afford.

withdrawal and RedBROU has a 200 USD limit. As *cambios* do not charge commission, at current rates it makes more sense to withdraw dollars and exchange them into pesos than to withdraw pesos directly.

ATM withdrawal fees The withdrawal fees in Uruguay vary but you can expect to pay 5-6 USD per withdrawal to the Uruguayan bank, as well as your own bank fees.

Which ATMs? Use the terminals that have Cirrus/Maestro/Link/VISA and other stickers on them. The other terminals are for Uruguayan card holders only.

Having trouble withdrawing money? Try these ATM hacks

These may seem really weird, but some of them have actually worked for readers[48].

- If you want pesos from a BROU ATM, tell the machine your account is in pesos, even though it's not.
- If you want dollars from a BROU ATM, tell the machine your account is in dollars.
- At a Banred ATM, choose Visa International or Mastercard International as your network, depending on your card. Never choose Visa Uruguay or Mastercard Uruguay.
- If you can't withdraw money on a debit card, try withdrawing from checking and choose 200 USD, not the maximum 300 USD.
- If the English instructional menu gives you an error code and says the selected amount isn't available, try the Spanish menu.
- Try withdrawing between 11am and 7pm.

Get your VAT off when paying by international credit card

As a tourist when you use your international credit card in Uruguay you automatically get your tax back in restaurants and on hire cars. There is no hotel tax for non-Uruguayans. This benefit has been rolled over year after year. The Guru'Guay website[49] will give you the latest status.

---

48 Thanks to Mark Mercer of Uruguay Expat Life for sharing some of these apparently crazy hacks
49 www.guruguay.com/use-credit-card-get-vat-off

Tipping

Tipping in Uruguay is voluntary and appreciated.

Restaurants Tip 10% of your bill or round-up. If service has been poor, don't tip. In general restaurants do not include a service charge though in a touristy venue you may see it. The *cubierto* charged in some restaurants is a cover charge which includes the cost of bread and sundries. This charge is dying out but you'll come across it and there's no getting away from it, other than to eat elsewhere (don't think you can just send the bread basket back, it don't work that way. Harrumph.).

Taxis Uruguayans do not tip taxi drivers as a rule. If you want to, a 10% tip is appreciated, as is rounding-up.

Gas station attendants No petrol station in Uruguay is self-service. As well as pump gas, attendants will wash your windscreen, fill your windscreen wiper bottle and put air in your tyres on request. A ten-peso tip is appreciated for any service beyond pumping gas.

Baggage handlers & porters I recommend carrying spare one dollar bills (or twenty-peso notes) for tipping in hotels and at the airport.

Street parking attendants Informal parking attendants have been a feature of Montevideo since the 1930s. When you return to your car, tip ten pesos. If you have just parked for a few minutes a couple of coins is fine. At night, tip more generously, such as a twenty-peso note.

Acknowledgments

Sylvana Cabrera Nahson for her support and generosity and convincing me to produce a print version of *The Guru'Guay Guide to Montevideo* when I had only been planning digital.

Liber Pisciottano and Nicolas Cappellini of Montevideo Wine Experience for their time and advice chewing over the different options of vineyards to recommend and for introducing me to wine-makers. And for their selection of Uruguay's best twenty wines. Viviana del Rio and Claudio Angelotti of Bodegas del Uruguay for providing their top budget wine picks.

Just when I was despairing of finding great eateries to recommend off season, I was introduced to chef Laura Rosano, leader in the slow food movement and author of two beautiful recipe books on native fruits and Ale Sequeira, local food expert and journalist. Because of them, you dear readers are going to have some of the most exciting culinary experiences possible in Uruguay.

Alejandro Bauer Arrillaga for opening the doors of the interior of Uruguay to me. Carmen Passarella Castellini and Marina Cantera Nebel, former president and current president of the Uruguayan association for rural tourism for advising me and introducing me to estancia owners. The Department of Tourism of Florida for the invitation to visit Florida.

My beach informants Alicia Barbitta in Punta del Este, Vero Iglesias on La Paloma and Carlota De Micheli in La Pedrera.

Fernando Alvarez of the the Fiestas Uruguayas website for generously sharing his lovingly-curated database of all the festivals in Uruguay and selecting the best events.

My friends in Uruguay who regularly get grilled for tidbits that end up in some shape or form on Guru'Guay. I hope I have not ruined too many secret spots. My guests at Casa Sarandi, wonderful folks who are generally psyched to go check out a new place for me. The readers of Guru'Guay and the Uruguay Expat Community Facebook group for sharing Uru-life hacks.

My old university friend, Lesley Davies-Evans, for coming up with the name Guru'Guay. It always makes English-speakers laugh. And that's the best.

Ace artist Matias Bervejillo for taking my ideas and turning them into the most delightful cover design ever. Lori Nordstrom for being my occasional sounding board. The Government of Montevideo for making the Torres Garcia font freely available for public use.

And of course, thank you to my partner Sergio Meresman—'the man behind the Guru'.

Photography credits

I am very grateful to Indrasish Banerjee, who takes photos for the Guru'Guay website and the other photographers, many of them professional, who share their wonderful work on Flickr.com. Thank you for your generosity and for helping bring Uruguay to life for the readers of this guide.

Punta del Diablo	Leo Alvarez
Santa Teresa National Park	Marcelo Campi
Cabo Polonio	Indrashish Banerjee
La Paloma	Jimmy Baikovicius
Jose Ignacio	Indrashish Banerjee
La Barra	Rodrigo Soldon
Punta del Este	Jimmy Baikovicius
Punta Ballena	Joao Vicente
Whale-watching	Remco Douma
Atlantida	Juan Pablo Colasso
El Pinar	Marcelo Campi
Montevideo	Kumsval
Colonia del Sacramento	Philip Choi
Estancia El Ceibo	Karen A Higgs
San Pedro de Timote	Karen A Higgs
Estancia Los Platanos	Karen A Higgs
Estancia Yvytu Itaty	Karen A Higgs
Estancia La Paz	Karen A Higgs
Estancia La Estiria	Alois Staudacher
Caballos de Luz	Violeta Carchak
Wine country	Indrashish Banerjee
East coast	Indrashish Banerjee
Practical tips	Marcelo Campi
Holidays & festivals	Indrashish Banerjee
Public transport	Jonas de Carvalho
Personal safety	Oatsy 40
Staying healthy	Hernan Piñera

About the author

Karen A Higgs grew up in the South Wales Valleys. At 22 she found herself stranded in Mexico City airport with just a pocket Spanish dictionary for company. Since then she's lived most of her life in Latin America. She sang 60s covers in a psychedelic rock bar in Costa Rica. In Buenos Aires, she impressed her teenage English-language students by riding a 500 cc motorbike around town. In 2000, she moved to Uruguay to run the communications team of an international non-profit. Now the owner of an award-winning guesthouse in Montevideo's Old City, pleas from grateful guests to share her insider information more widely inspired the popular Guru'Guay website in 2014 and *The Guru'Guay Guide to Montevideo* in 2016. In November 2017, after scouring the country for over a year, she published *The Guru'Guay Guide to Uruguay: Beaches, Ranches & Wine Country*.

The Guru'Guay Guide to Montevideo

This 140-page guidebook is the only indepth city guide in English to the capital of Uruguay. It includes chapters on architectural delights, art galleries, historic cafés, carnival, tango and eight pages on live music—but what readers love most is the focus on culture and society in Uruguay as a whole which covers topics like:

- **history** How did this tiny country get to be so progressive? Your burning questions answered.
- **the Uruguayan character**, a chapter of entirely personal anecdotes that illustrate that Uruguayans from presidents to petty thieves are friendly and down-to-earth
- expressions only used in Uruguay and what they mean
- **Uruguayan films** to watch **and albums** to listen to **and books** to read before you come.

Buy the two guides as a set, and you have everything you need to painlessly plan your entire holiday in Uruguay based on the essential tips only a long-time insider can give you.

No painful ploughing through a traditional guidebook. The Guru'Guay Guides are easy reading, more like chatting with a friend.

Printed in Great Britain
by Amazon